THE MARTIAL ADVENTURES
OF HENRY AND ME

THE MACMILLAN COMPANY
NEW YORK · BOSTON · CHICAGO · DALLAS
ATLANTA · SAN FRANCISCO

MACMILLAN & CO., LIMITED
LONDON · BOMBAY · CALCUTTA
MELBOURNE

THE MACMILLAN CO. OF CANADA, LTD.
TORONTO

The Martial Adventures of Henry and Me

BY

WILLIAM ALLEN WHITE
Author of "A Certain Rich Man," etc.

WITH ILLUSTRATIONS BY
TONY SARG

New York
THE MACMILLAN COMPANY
1918

All rights reserved

COPYRIGHT, 1918
BY THE MACMILLAN COMPANY

Set up and electrotyped. Published, April, 1918

CONTENTS

ILLUSTRATIONS

Illustrations

THE MARTIAL ADVENTURES
OF HENRY AND ME

CHAPTER I

IN WHICH WE BEGIN OUR SENTIMENTAL JOURNEY

BY rights Henry, being the hero of this story, should be introduced in the first line. But really there isn't so much to say about Henry — Henry J. Allen for short, as we say in Kansas — Henry J. Allen, editor and owner of the Wichita *Beacon.* And to make the dramatis personæ complete, we may consider me as the editor of the Emporia *Gazette,* and the two of us as short, fat, bald, middle-aged, inland Americans, from fresh water colleges in our youth and arrived at New York by way of an often devious, yet altogether happy route, leading through politics where it was rough going and unprofitable for years; through business where we still find it easy to sign, possible to float and hard to pay a ninety-day note, and through two country towns; one somewhat less than one hundred thousand population, and Emporia slightly above ten thousand.

We are discovered in the prologue to the play in New York City wearing our new silk suits to give New York a treat on a hot August day. Not that we or any one else ever wears silk suits in any Wichita or Emporia; silk suits are bought by Wichita people and Emporians all over the earth to paralyse the natives of the various New Yorks.

In our pockets we hold commissions from the American Red Cross. These commissions are sending us to Europe as inspectors with a view to publicity later, one to speak for the Red Cross, the other to write for it in America. We have been told by the Red Cross authorities in Washington that we shall go immediately to the front in France and that it will be necessary to have the protective colouring of some kind of an army uniform. The curtain rises on a store in 43rd Street in New York — perhaps the " Palace " or the " Hub " or the " Model " or the " Army and Navy," where a young man is trying to sell us a khaki coat, and shirt and trousers for $17.48. And at that it seems a lot of money to pay for a rig which can be worn at most only two months. But we compromise by making him throw in an-

And at that it seems a lot of money to pay for a rig
which can be worn at most only two months

other shirt and a service hat and we take the lot
for $17.93 and go away holding in low esteem
the " pride, pomp and circumstance of glorious
war " as exemplified by these military duds.   In
our hearts as we go off at R. U. E. will be seen
a hatred for uniforms as such, and particularly
for phoney uniforms that mean nothing and cost
$18.00 in particular.

And then, with a quick curtain, the good ship
Espagne, a French liner, is discovered in New
York harbour the next day with Henry and me
aboard her, trying to distinguish as she crawfishes
out of the dock, the faces of our waving friends
from the group upon the pier.

The good ship *Espagne* is all steamed up and
scooting through the night, with two or three
hundred others of the cast of characters aboard;
and there is Europe and the war in the cast of
characters, and the Boche, and Fritzie and the
Hun, that diabolic trinity of evil, and just back
of the boat on the scenery of the first act, splat-
tered like guinea freckles all over the American
map for three thousand miles north, south, east
and west, are a thousand replicas of Wichita
and Emporia.   So it really is not of arms and
the man that this story is written, nor of Henry
and me, and the war; but it is the eternal Wichita

and Emporia in the American heart that we shall celebrate hereinafter as we unfold our tale. Of course, that makes it provincial. And people living in New York or Boston, or Philadelphia (but not Chicago, for half of the people there have just come to town and the other half is just ready to leave town) may not understand this story. For in some respects New York is larger than Wichita and Emporia; but not so much larger; for mere numbers of population amount to little. There is always an angle of the particular from which one can see it as a part of the universal; and seen properly the finite is always infinite. And that brings us back naturally to Henry and me, looking out at the scurrying stars in the ocean as we hurried through the black night on the good ship *Espagne*. We had just folded away a fine Sunday dinner, a French Sunday dinner, beginning with onion soup which was strange; and as ominous of our journey into the Latin world as a blast of trumpets opening a Wagnerian overture. Indeed that onion soup was threaded through our whole trip like a motif. Our dinner that night ended in cheese and everything. It was our first meal aboard the boat. During two or three courses, we had considered the value of food as a two-way commodity

— going down and coming up — but later in the dinner we ordered our food on its merits as a one-way luxury, with small thought as to its other uses.   So we leaned against the rail in the night and thought large thoughts about Wichita and Emporia.

Here we were, two middle-aged men, nearing fifty years, going out to a ruthless war without our wives.   We had packed our own valises at the hotel that very morning in fear and trembling. We realized that probably we were leaving half our things in closets and drawers and were taking the wrong things with us, and checking the right things in our trunks at our hotels in New York. We had some discussion about our evening clothes, and on a toss-up had decided to take our tails and leave our dinner coats in the trunks. But we didn't know why we had abandoned our dinner coats.   We had no accurate social knowledge of those things.   Henry boasted that his wife had taught him a formula that would work in the matter of white or black ties with evening clothes.   But it was all complicated with white vests and black vests and sounded like a corn remedy; yet it was the only sartorial foundation we had.   And there we were with land out of sight, without a light visible on the boat, standing in the black of night leaning over the rail, looking at the stars in the water, and wondering silently whether we had packed our best cuff buttons, "with which to harry our foes," or whether we might have to win the war in our $17.93 uniforms, and we both thought and admitted our shame, that our wives would think we had been extravagant in putting so much money into those uniforms. The admirable French dinner which we had just enveloped, seemed a thousand miles away. It was a sad moment and our thoughts turned naturally to home.

"Fried chicken, don't you suppose?" sighed Henry.

"And mashed potatoes, and lots of thick cream gravy!" came from the gloom beside him.

"And maybe lima beans," he speculated.

"And a lettuce salad with thousand island dressing, I presume!" came out of the darkness.

"And apple dumpling — green apple dumpling with hard sauce," welled up from Henry's heavy heart. It was a critical moment. If it had kept on that way we would have got off the boat, and trudged back home through a sloppy ocean, and let the war take care of itself. Then Henry's genius rose. Henry is the world's greatest kidder. Give him six days' immunity in Germany, and let him speak in Berlin, Munich, Dresden, Leipsic and Cologne and he would kid the divine right of kings out of Germany and the kaiser on to the Chautauqua circuit, reciting his wrongs and his reminiscences!

Henry, you may remember, delivered the Roosevelt valedictory at the Chicago Republican convention in 1912, when he kidded the standpat crowd out of every Republican state in the union but two at the election. Possibly you don't like that word kid. But it's in the dictionary, and there's no other word to describe Henry's talent. He is always jamming the allegro into the adagio. And that night in the encircling gloom on the boat as we started on our martial adventures he began kidding the ocean. His idea was that he would get Wichita to vote bonds for one that would bring tide water to Main Street. He didn't want a big ocean — just a kind of an oceanette with a seating capacity of five thousand square miles was his idea, and when he had done with his phantasie, the doleful dumps that rose at the psychical aroma of the hypothetical fried chicken and mashed potatoes of our dream, had vanished.

And so we fell to talking about our towns. It seems that we had each had the same experience. Henry declared that, from the day it was known he was going to Europe for the Red Cross, the town had set him apart; he was somewhat like the doomed man in a hanging and people were always treating him with distinguished consideration. He had a notion that Henry Lassen, the town boomer, had the memorial services all worked out — who would sing " How Sleep the Brave," who would play Chopin's funeral march on the pipe organ, who would deliver the eulogy and just what leading advertiser they would send around to the *Eagle,* his hated contemporary, to get the Murdocks to print the eulogy in full and on the first page! Henry employs an alliterative head writer on the *Beacon,* and we wondered whether he had decided to use " Wichita Weeps," or " State Stands Sorrowing." If he used the latter, it would make two lines and that would require a deck head. We could not decide, so we began talking of serious things.

How quickly time has rolled the film since those early autumn days when the man who went to France was a hero in his town's eyes. Processions and parades and pageants interminable have passed down America's main streets, all headed for France. And what proud pageants they were! Walking at the head of the line were the little limping handful of veterans of the Civil

War. After them came the middle-aged huskies
of the Spanish War, and then, so very young, so
boyish and so very solemn, came the soldiers for
the great war — the volunteers, the National
Guard, the soldiers of the new army; half ac-
coutred, clad in nondescript uniforms, but proud
and incorrigibly young. There had been ban-
quets the week before, and speeches and flag ritu-
als in public, but the night before, there had been
tears and good-byes across the land. And all this
in a few weeks; indeed it began during the long
days in which we two sailed through the gulf
stream, we two whose departure from our towns
had seemed such a bold and hazardous adventure.
When one man leaves a town upon an unusual en-
terprise, it may look foolhardy; but when a hundred leave upon the same adventure, it seems commonplace. The danger in some way seems to be
divided by the numbers. Yet in truth, numbers
often multiply the danger. There was little danger for Henry and me on the good ship *Espagne*
with Red Cross stenographers and nurses and ambulance drivers and Y. M. C. A. workers. No
particular advantage would come to the German
arms by torpedoing us. But as the *Espagne,* carrying her peaceful passengers, all hurrying to Europe on merciful errands, passed down the river

and into the harbour that afternoon, we had seen a great grey German monster passenger boat, an interned leviathan of the sea in her dock. We had been told of how cunningly the Germans had scuttled her; how they had carefully relaid electric wires so that every strand had to be retraced to and from its source, how they had turned the course of water pipes, all over the ship, how they had drawn bolts and with blow-pipes had rotted nuts and rods far in the dark places of the ship's interior, how they had scientifically disarranged her boilers so that they would not make steam, and as we saw the German boat looming up, deck upon deck, a floating citadel, with her bristling guns, we thought what a prize she would be when she put out to sea loaded to the guards with those handsome boys whom we had been seeing hustling about the country as they went to their training camps. Even to consider these things gave us a feeling of panic, and the recollection of the big boat in the dock began to bring the war to us, more vividly than it had come before. And then our first real martial adventure happened, thus:

As we leaned over the rail that first night talking of many things, in the blackness, without a glimmer from any porthole, with the decks as dark as Egypt, the ship shot ahead at twenty knots an hour. In peace times it would be regarded as a crazy man's deed, to go whizzing along at full speed without lights. Henry had taken two long puffs on his cigar when out from the murk behind us came a hand that tapped his shoulder, and then a voice spoke:

" You'll have to put out that cigar, sir. A submarine could see that five miles on a night like this!"

So Henry doused his light, and the war came right home to us.

The next day was uniform day on the boat, and the war came a bit nearer to us than ever. Scores of good people who had come on the boat in civilian clothes, donned their uniforms that second day; mostly Red Cross or Y. M. C. A. or American ambulance or Field Service uniforms. We did not don our uniforms, though Henry believed that we should at least have a dress rehearsal. The only regular uniforms on board were worn by a little handful of French soldiers, straggling home from a French political mission to America, and these French soldiers were the only passengers on the boat who had errands to France connected with the destructive side of the war. So not until the uniforms blazed out gorgeously did we realize what an elaborate and important business had sprung up in the reconstructive side of war. Here we saw a whole ship's company — hundreds of busy and successful men and women, one of scores and scores of ship's companies like it, that had been hurrying across the ocean every few days for three years, devoted not to trading upon the war, not to exploiting the war, not even to expediting the business of " the gentle art of murdering," but devoted to saving the waste of war!

As the days passed, and " we sailed and we sailed," a sort of denatured pirate craft armed to the teeth with healing lotions to massage the wrinkled front of war, Henry kept picking at the ocean. It was his first transatlantic voyage; for like most American men, he kept his European experiences in his wife's name. So the ocean bothered him. He understood a desert or a drouth, but here was a tremendous amount of unnecessary and unaccountable water. It was a calm, smooth, painted ocean, and as he looked at it for a long time one day, Henry remarked wearily: " The town boosters who secured this ocean for this part of the country rather overdid the job!"

One evening, looking back at the level floor of the ocean stretching illimitably into the golden

" You'll have to put out that cigar, sir "

sunset, he mused: " They have a fine country
here. You kind of like the lay of it, and there
is plenty of nice sightly real estate about — it's a
gently rolling country, uneven and something like
College Hill in Wichita, but there's got to be a
lot of money spent draining it; you can tell that
at a glance, if the fellow gets anywhere with his
proposition!"

A time always comes in a voyage, when men
and women begin to step out as individuals from
the mass. With us it was the Red Cross stenographers and the American Ambulance boys
who first ceased being ladyships and lordships and
took their proper places in the cosmos. They
were a gay lot — and young. And human nature
is human nature. So the decks began to clutter
up with boys and girls intensely interested in ex-
ploring each other's lives. It is after all the most
wonderful game in the world. And while the
chaperon fluttered about more or less, trying to
shoo the girls off the dark decks at night, and
while public opinion on the boat made eminently
proper rules against young women in the smoking room, still young blood did have its way,
which really is a good way; better than we think,
perhaps, who look back in cold blood and old
blood. And by the token of our years it was

brought to us that war is the game of youth. We were two middle-aged old coots — though still in our forties and not altogether blind to a pretty face — and yet the oldest people on the boat. Even the altruistic side of war is the game of youth.

Perhaps it is the other way around, and maybe youth is the only game in the world worth playing and that the gains of youth, service and success and follies and failures, are only the chips and counters. We were brought to these conclusions more or less by a young person, a certain Miss Ingersoll, or perhaps her name only sounded like that; for we called her the Eager Soul. And she was a pretty girl, too — American pretty: Red hair — lots of blowy, crinkly red hair that was always threatening to souse her face and ears; blue eyes of the serious kind and a colour that gave us the impression that she did exercises and could jab a punching bag. Indeed before we met her, we began betting on the number of hours it would take her to tell us that she took a cold plunge every morning. Henry expected the statement on the second day; as a matter of fact it came late on the first day! She was that kind. But there was no foolishness about her. She was a nurse — a Red Cross nurse, and she made it

clear that she had no illusions about men; we sus-
pected that she had seen them cut up and knew
their innermost secrets! Nevertheless she was
tremendously interesting, and because she, too,
was from the middle west, and possibly because
she realized that we accepted her for what she
was, she often paced the rounds of the deck between us. We teased her more or less about a
young doctor of the Johns Hopkins unit who
sometimes hovered over her deck chair and a certain Gilded Youth — every boat-load has its
Gilded Youth — whose father was president of
so many industrial concerns, and the vice-president of so many banks and trust companies that
it was hard to look at the boy without blinking at
his gilding. Henry was betting on the Gilded
Youth; so the young doctor fell to me. For the
first three or four days during which we kept
fairly close tab on their time, the Doctor had the
Gilded Youth beaten two hours to one. Henry
bought enough lemonade for me and smoking
room swill of one sort and another to start his little old Wichita ocean. But it was plain that the
Gilded Youth interested her. And in a confidential moment filled with laughter and chaff and
chatter she told us why: " He's patronizing me.
I mean he doesn't know it, and he thinks I don't

know it; but that's what he's doing. I interest him as a social specimen. I mean — I'm a bug and he likes to take me up and examine me. I think I'm the first 'Co-ed' he ever has seen; the first girl who voted and didn't let her skirts sag and still loved good candy! I mean that when he found in one half hour that I knew he wore nine dollar neckties and that I was for Roosevelt, the man nearly expired; he was that puzzled! I'm not quite the type of working girl whom Heaven protects and he chases, but — I mean I think he is wondering just how far Heaven really will protect my kind! When he decides," she confided in a final burst of laughter, and tucking away her overflowing red hair, " I may have to slap him — I mean don't you know —"

And we did know. And being in his late forties Henry began tantalizing me with odds on the Gilded Youth. He certainly was a beautiful boy — tall, chestnut haired, clean cut, and altogether charming. He played Brahms and Irving Berlin with equal grace on the piano in the women's lounge on the ship and an amazing game of stud poker with the San Francisco boys in the smoking room. And it was clear that he regarded the Eager Soul as a social adventure somewhat higher than his mother's social secretary — but of the

She often paced the rounds of the deck between us

same class.   He was returning from a furlough,
to drive his ambulance in France, and the Doctor
was going out to join his unit somewhere in
France down near the Joan of Arc country.   He
told us shyly one day, as we watched the wake
of the ship together, that he was to be stationed
at an old chateau upon whose front is carved in
stone, " I serve because I am served! "   When
he did not repeat the motto we knew that it had
caught him.   He had been at home working on
a germ problem connected with army life, hardly
to be mentioned in the presence of Mrs. Boffin,
and he was forever casually discussing his diffi-
culties with the Eager Soul; and a stenographer,
who came upon the two at their tête-à-tête one
day, ran to the girls in the lounge and gasped,
" My Lord, Net, if you'd a heard it, you'd a
jumped off the boat! "

As the passenger list began to resolve itself
into familiar faces and figures and friends we
became gradually aware of a pair of eyes — a
pair of snappy black, female, French eyes.
Speaking broadly and allowing for certain Emporia and Wichita exceptions, eyes were no treat
to us.   Yet we fell to talking blithely of those
eyes.   Henry said if he had to douse his cigar
on deck at night, the captain should make the

Princess wear dimmers at night or stay indoors.
We were not always sure she was a Princess.
At times she seemed more like a Duchess or a
Countess, according to her clothes. We never
had seen such clothes! And millinery! We
were used to Broadway; Michigan Avenue did
not make us shy, and Henry had been in the
South. But these clothes and the hats and the
eyes — all full dress — were too many for us.
And we fell to speculating upon exactly what
would happen on Main Street and Commercial
Street in Wichita and Emporia if the Duchess
could sail down there in full regalia. Henry's
place at table was where he got the full voltage
of the eyes every time the Princess switched them
on. And whenever he reached for the water and
gulped it down, one could know he had been jolted
behind his ordinary resisting power. And he
drank enough to float a ship! As we wended
our weary way over the decks during the long
lonely hours of the voyage, we fell to theorizing
about those eyes and we concluded that they were
Latin — Latin chiefly engaged in the business of
being female eyes. It was a new show to us.
Our wives and mothers had voted at city elections
for over thirty years and had been engaged for
a generation in the business of taming their hus-

bands; saving the meat from dinner for the hash
for breakfast, and betimes for diversion, working
in their clubs for the good of their towns; and
their eyes had visions in them, not sex.   So these
female eyes showed us a mystery!   And each of
us in his heart decided to investigate the phe-
nomena.   And on the seventh day we laid off
from our work and called it good.   We had met
the Princess.   Our closer view persuaded us that
she might be thirty-five but probably was forty,
though one early morning in a passage way we
met her when she looked fifty, wan and sad and
weary, but still flashing her eyes.   And then one
fair day, she turned her eyes from us for ever.
This is what happened to me.   But Henry himself may have been the hero of the episode.   Anyway, one of us was walking the deck with the
Countess investigating the kilowat power of the
eyes.   He was talking of trivial things, possibly
telling the lady fair of the new ten-story Beacon
Building or of Henry Ganse's golf score on the
Emporia Country Club links — anyway something of broad, universal human interest.   But
those things seemed to pall on her.   So he tried
her on the narrow interests that engage the women
at home — the suffrage question; the matter of
the eight-hour day and the minimum wage for

women; and national prohibition. These things left her with no temperature. She was cold; she even shivered, slightly, but gracefully withal, as she went swinging along on her toes, her silk sweater clinging like an outer skin to her slim lithe body, walking like a girl of sixteen. And constantly she was at target practice with her eyes with all her might and main. She managed to steer the conversation to a place where she could bemoan the cruel war; and ask what the poor women would do. Her Kansas partner suggested that life would be broader and better for women after the war, because they would have so much more important a part to do than before in the useful work of the world. "Ah, yes," she said, "perhaps so. But with the men all gone what shall we do when we want to be petted?" She made two sweet unaccented syllables of petted in her ingénue French accent and added: "For you know women were made to be pet-ted." There was a bewildered second under the machine gun fire of the eyes when her companion considered seriously her theory. He had never cherished such a theory before. But he was seeing a new world, and this seemed to be one of the pleasant new things in it — this theory of the woman requiring to be pet-ted!

Then the French Colonel hove in sight and she said: "Oh, yes — come on, Col-o-nel" — making three unaccented syllables of the word — "and we shall have une femme sandweech." She gave the Colonel her arm. The miserable Kansan had not thought to take it, being busy with the Beacon Building or the water hazard at the Emporia Country Club, and then, as the Col-o-nel took her arm she lifted the Eyes to the stupid clod of a Kansan and switched on all the joyous incandescence of her lamps as she said, addressing the Frenchman but gazing sweetly at the American, "Col-o-nel, will you please carry my books?" They must have weighed six or eight ounces! And she shifted them to the Col-o-nel as though they weighed a ton!

So the Kansan walked wearily to the smoking room to find his mate. They two then and there discussed the woman proposition in detail and drew up strong resolutions of respect for the Wichita and Emporia type, the American type that carries its own books and burdens and does not require of its men a silly and superficial chivalry and does not stimulate it by the everlasting lure of sex! Men may die for the Princess and her kind and enjoy death. We were willing that they should. We evinced no desire to impose our kultur on others. But after that day on the deck the Princess lost her lure for Henry and me! So we went to the front stoop of the boat and watched the Armenians drill. A great company of them was crowded in the steerage and all day long, with a sergeant major, they went through the drill. They were returning to Europe to fight with the French army and avenge the wrongs of their people. When they tired of drilling, they danced, and when they tired of dancing, they sang. It was queer music for civilized ears, the Armenian songs they sang. It was written on a barbaric scale with savage cadences and broken time; but it was none the less sweet for being weird. It had the charm and freedom of the desert in it, and was as foreign as the strange brown faces that lifted toward us as they sang.

"What is that music?" asked the Kansans of a New England boy in khaki who had been playing Greig that day for them on the piano. "That," nodded the youth toward the Armenians. "Oh, that — why that's the 'Old Oaken Bucket!'" His face did not relax and he went away whistling! So there we were. The Col-o-nel and the lady with their idea on the woman question, the Armenians with their bizarré

" Col-o-nel, will you please carry my books?"

music, the Yankee with his freaky humour, and
the sedentary gold dust twins from Kansas, and
a great boat-load of others like them in their
striking differences of ideals and notions, all hurrying across the world to help in the great fight
for democracy which, in its essence, is only the
right to live in the world, each man, each cult,
each race, each blood and each nation after its
own kind.   And about all the war involves is the
right to live, and to love one's own kind of
women, one's own kind of music, one's own kind
of humour, one's own kind of philosophy; knowing that they are not perfect and understanding
their limitations; trusting to time and circumstance to bring out the fast colours of life in the
eternal wash.   Thinking thoughts like these that
night, Henry's bunk-mate could not sleep.   So
he slipped on a grey overcoat over his pajamas
and put on a grey hat and grey rubber-soled shoes,
and went out on deck into the hot night that falls
in the gulf stream in summer.   It was the murky
hour before dawn and around and around the
deck he paced noiselessly, a grey, but hardly gaunt
spectre in the night.   The deck chairs were filled
with sleepers from the berths below decks.   At
last, wearying of his rounds, the spectre stopped
to gaze over the rail at the water and the stars

when he heard this from a deck chair behind him, "Wake up, Net — for God's sake wake up!" whispered a frightened woman's voice. "There's that awful thing again that scared me so awhile ago!"

Even at the latter end of the journey the ocean interested us. An ocean always seems so unreasonable to inlanders. And that morning when there was "a grey mist on the sea's face and a grey dawn breaking," Henry came alongside and looked at the seascape, all twisting and writhing and tossing and billowing, up and down and sideways. He also looked at his partner who was gradually growing pale and wan and weary. And Henry heard this: "She's on a bender; she's riz about ten feet during the night. I guess there's been rain somewhere up near the headwaters or else the fellow took his finger out of the hole in the dyke. Anyway, she'll be out of her banks before breakfast. I don't want any breakfast; I'm going to bed for the day." And he went.

During the day Henry brought the cheerful information that the Doctor was down and that the Eager Soul and the Gilded Youth were wearing out the deck. Henry also added that her slapping was scheduled for that night.

" Has her hair slopped over yet? "   This from me.

" No," answered Henry, " but it's getting crinklier and crinklier and she looks pinker and pinker, and prettier and prettier, and you ought to see her in her new purple sweater.   She sprang that on the boat this afternoon!   It's laying 'em out in swaths! "   Henry's affinity was afraid to turn off his back.   But he turned a pale face toward his side-kick and whispered: " Henry, you tell her," he gulped before going on, " that if she can't find anyone else to slap, there's a man down here who can't fight back! "

A sense of security comes to one who churns along seven days on a calm sea on an eventless voyage.   And the French, by easy-going ways, stimulate that sense of security; we had heard weird stories of boat-drills at daybreak, of midnight alarms and of passengers sleeping on deck in their life preservers, and we were prepared for the thrills which Wichita and Emporia expected us to have.   They never came.   One afternoon, seven or eight days out, we had notice at noon that we would try on our life preservers that afternoon.   The life preservers were thrown on our beds by the stewards and at three o'clock each passenger appeared beside the life-boat assigned

to him, donned his life-belt which gave him a
ridiculously stuffed appearance, answered to a
roll-call, guyed those about him after the manner
of old friends, and waited for something else.
It never came. The ship's officers gradually
faded from the decks and the passengers, after
standing around foolishly for a time, disappeared
one by one into their cabins and bloomed out
again with their life-belts moulted!   That was the
last we heard of the boat-drill or the life-belts.
The French are just that casual.

But one evening at late twilight the ship went
a-flutter over a grisly incident that brought us
close up to the war. We were gathered in the
dusk looking at a sailing ship far over to the
south — a mere speck on the horizon's edge.
Signals began to twinkle from her and we felt
our ship give a lurch and turn north zigzagging
at full speed. The signals of the sailing ship
were distress signals, but we sped away from her
as fast as our engines would take us, for, though
her signals may have been genuine, also they
may have been a U-boat lure. Often the Germans have used the lure of distress signals on a
sailing ship and when a rescuer has appeared, the
U-boat has sent to death the Good Samaritan of

the sea! It is awful. But the German has put mercy off the sea!

Some way the average man goes back to his home environment for his moral standards, and that night as we walked the deck, Henry broke out with this: " I've been thinking about this U-boat business; how it would be if we had the German's job. I have been trying to think if there is any one in Wichita who could go out and run a U-boat the way these Germans run U-boats, and I've been trying to imagine him sitting on the front porch of the Country Club or down at the Elks Club talking about it; telling how he lured the captain of a ship by his distress signal to come to the rescue of a sinking ship and then destroyed the rescuer, and I've been trying to figure out how the fellows sitting around him would take it. They'd get up and leave. He would be outcast as unspeakable and no brag or bluff or blare of victory would gloss over his act. We simply don't think the German way. We have a loyalty to humanity deeper than our patriotism. There are certain things self-respecting men can't do and live in Wichita. But there seem to be no restrictions in Germany. The U-boat captain using the distress signal as a lure probably holds about such a place in his home town as Charley Carey, our banker, or Walter Innes, our dry goods man. He is doubtless a leading citizen of some German town; doubtless a kind father, a good husband and maybe a pillar of the church. And I suppose town and home and church will applaud him when he goes back to Germany to brag about his treachery. In Wichita, town and home and church would be ashamed of Charley Carey and Walter Innes if they came back to brag about killing men who were lured to death by responding to the call of distress."

And so, having disposed of the psychology of the enemy, we turned in for the night. We were entering the danger zone and the night was hot. A few passengers slept on deck; but most of the ship's company went to their cabins. We didn't seem to be afraid. We presumed that our convoy would appear in the morning. But when it failed to appear we assumed that there was no danger. No large French passenger boat had been sunk by the Germans; this fact we heard a dozen times that day. It soothed us. The day passed without bringing our convoy. Again we went to bed, realizing rather clearly that the French do take things casually; and believing

firmly that the convoys would come with the
dawn.   But dawn came and brought no convoy.
We seemed to be nearing land.   The horizon was
rarely without a boat.   The day grew bright.
We were almost through the danger zone.   We
went to lunch a gay lot, all of us; but we hurried
back to the deck; not uneasily, not in fear, understand, but just to be on deck, looking landward.
And then at two o'clock it appeared.   Far off in
the northeast was a small black dot in the sky.
It looked like a seabird; but it grew.   In ten minutes the whole deck was excited.   Every glass
was focused on the growing black spot.   And
then it loomed up the size of a baseball; it showed
colour, a dull yellow in the distance and then it
swelled and took form and glowed brighter and
came rushing toward us, as large as a moon, as
large as a barrel, and then we saw its outlines,
and it came swooping over us, a great beautiful
golden thing and the whole deck burst into cheers.
It was our convoy, a dirigible balloon — vivid
golden yellow, trimmed with blue!   How fair it
seemed.   How graceful and how surely and how
powerfully it circled about the ship like a great
hovering bird, and how safe we felt; and as
we cheered and cheered the swirling, glowing,
beautiful thing, we knew how badly frightened

we really had been.   With danger gone, the tension lifted and we read the fear in our hearts.   A torpedo boat destroyer came lumbering across the sky line.   It also was to convoy us, but it had a most undramatic entrance; and besides we had sighted land.   The deck cheered easily, so we cheered the land.   And everyone ran about exclaiming to everyone else about the wonder and splendour of the balloon, and everyone took pictures of everyone else and promised to send prints, and the land waxed fat and loomed large and hospitable while Henry paced the deck with his hands clasped reflectively behind him.   He was deeply moved and language didn't satisfy him much.   Finally he took his fellow Kansan by the arm and pointed to the magnificence of the hovering spectre in yellow and blue that circled about the ship:

"Bill," he said, solemnly, "isn't she a peach!" He paused, then from his heart he burst out: "'How beautiful upon the mountain are the feet of them that bring glad tidings!' I wish the fellows in Wichita could get this thing for the wheat show!"

And thus we came to the shores of sunny France, a land that was to remind us over and over again of our own sunny land of Kansas.

We landed after dark. Every one was going
about vowing deathless friendship to every one
else, and so far as the stenographers and the ambulance boys were concerned, it came to Henry
and me that we meant it; for they were a fine
lot, just joyous, honest, brave young Americans
going out to do their little part in a big enter-
prise. While we were bidding good-bye to our
boys and girls, we kept a weather eye on the
Eager Soul. She had hooked the Gilded Youth
fairly deeply. He saw that her trunk came up
from the hold, but we noticed that while he was
gone, the Doctor showed up and went with her
to sort out her hand-baggage from the pile on the
deck. The gang plank was let down under a pair
of smoky torches. And the Gilded Youth had
paid a fine tip some place to be permitted to be
the first passenger off the boat that he might get
one of the two taxis in sight for the Eager Soul.
She followed him, but she made him let the Doctor come along. And so the drinks — lemon
squash and buttermilk — were equally on Henry
and me. We hurried down the gang plank after
the happy trio. They were young — so infi-
nitely and ineffably young, it seemed to us. And
the girl's face was flushed and joyous, and her
hair — why it didn't shake out and drown her

we never knew; certainly it surged out from under her hat like ripples of youth incarnate. We saw them stacking their valises in the taxi and over the taxi and around the taxi and the last we saw of her was when she bent out of the cab window and waved and smiled at us, two sedate old parties alone there in the crowd, with the French language rising to our ears as we teetered unsteadily into it.

What an adventure they were going into — what a new adventure, the new and beautiful adventure of youth, the old and inexplicable adventure of life! So we waved back at them so long as they were in sight, and the white handkerchief of the Eager Soul fluttered back from the disappearing cab. When it was gone, Henry turned to a sad-looking cabman with a sway-backed carriage and explained with much eloquence that we wanted him to haul us a la hotel France — toot sweet!

So we waved back at them so long as they were in
sight

CHAPTER II

BORDEAUX is the "Somewhere in France" from which cablegrams from passengers on the French liners usually are sent. This will be no news to the Germans, nor to Americans who read the advertisements of the French liners, but it may be news to Americans who receive the mysterious cablegrams "from a French port," after their friends have landed. It is a dear old town, mouldy, and weather-beaten, and mediaeval, this Bordeaux, with high, mysterious walls along the streets over which hang dusty branches of trees or vines sneaking mischievously out of bounds. A woe-begone trolley creaks through the narrow streets and heart-broken cabmen mourning over the mistakes of misspent lives, larrup disconsolate horses over stony streets as they creak and jog and wheeze ahead of the invisible crows that seem always to be hovering above ready to batten upon their rightful provender. For an hour in the morning before our train left for Paris we chartered one of the ramshackle cabs of the town and took in Bordeaux. It was vastly unlike either Emporia or Wichita, or anything in Kansas, or anything in America; or so far as that goes, to Henry and me, it was unlike anything else in the wide and beautiful world. "All this needs," said Henry, as he lolled back upon the moth-eaten cushions of the hack that banged its iron rims on the cobbles beneath us, and sent the thrill of it into our teeth, "all this needs is Mary Pickford and a player organ to be a good film!" The only thing we saw that made us homesick was the group of firemen in front of the engine house playing checkers or chess or something. But the town had an historic interest for us as the home of the Girondists of the French Revolution; so we looked up their monument and did proper reverence to them. They were moderate idealists who rose during the first year of the revolution; we thought them much like the Bull Moosers. So we did what homage we could to the Girondists who were run over by the revolutionary band wagon and sent to the guillotine during the Terror. For we knew; indeed into the rolly-poly necks of Henry and me, in our own politics, the

knife had bitten many times.   So we stood before
what seemed to be the proper monument with
sympathetic eyes and uncovered heads for a second before we took the train for Paris.

All day long we rode through the only peaceful part of France we were to see in our martial adventures.   It was fair and fat and smiling
— that France that lay between the river Gironde
and Paris, and all day we rode through its beauty
and its richness.   The thing which we missed
most from the landscape, being used to the American landscape, was the automobile.   We did not
see one in the day's journey.   In Kansas alone
there are 190,000 continually pervading the landscape.   We had yet to learn that there are no private automobiles in France, that the government
had commandeered all automobiles and that even
the taxis of Paris have but ten gallons of gasoline
a day allotted to each of them.   So we gazed at
the two-wheeled carts, the high, bony, strong
white oxen, the ribbons of roads, hard-surfaced
and beautiful, wreathing the gentle hills, and
longed for a car to make the journey past the fine
old chateaux that flashed in and out of our vision
behind the hills.   War was a million miles away
from the pastoral France that we saw coming up
from Bordeaux.

But in Paris war met us far out in the suburbs, where at dusk a great flock of airplanes from a training camp buzzed over us and sailed along with the train, distancing us and returning to play with us like big sportive birds. The train was filled with our shipmates from the boat and we all craned our necks from the windows to look at the wonderful sight of the air covey that fluttered above us. Even the Eager Soul, our delicious young person with her crinkly red hair and serious eyes, disconnected herself long enough from the Gilded Youth and the Young Doctor " for to admire and for to see," the airplanes.

But the airplanes gave us the day's first opportunity to talk to the Eager Soul. Until dusk the Gilded Youth had kept her in his donjon — a first class compartment jammed with hand-baggage, and where she had insisted that the Young Doctor should come also. We knew that without being told; also it was evident as we passed up and down the car aisle during the day that she was acting as a sort of human Baedeker to the Young Doctor, while the Gilded Youth, to whom chateaux and French countryside were an old, old story, sat by and hooted. But the airplanes pulled him out of his donjon keep and the Young

Doctor with him. He wasn't above showing the
Young Doctor how much a Gilded Youth really
knows about mechanics and airplanes, and we
slipped in and chatted with the Eager Soul. We
had a human interest in the contest between the
Gilded Youth and the Young Doctor, and a sport-
ing interest which centered in the daily score.
And we gathered this: That it was the Young
Doctor's day. For he was in France to help the
greatest cause in the world; and the Gilded Youth
affected to be in France — to enjoy the greatest
outdoor game in the world. But he had made it
plain that day to the Eager Soul that working
eighteen hours a day under shell fire, driving an
ambulance, was growing tame. He was going
back, of course, but he was thinking seriously of
the air service. The Doctor wanted no thrills.
He was willing to boil surgical instruments or
squirt disinfectant around kitchens to serve. And
the Eager Soul liked that attitude, though it was
obvious to us, that she was in the war game as a
bit of a sport and because it was too dull in her
Old Home Town, "somewhere in the United
States." And we knew also what she did not ad-
mit, even if she recognized it, that in the Old
Home Town, men of the sort to attract women of
her spirit and intelligence were scarce — and she

was out looking for her own Sir Galahad, as he went up and down the earth searching for the Holy Grail. The war to her, we knew, was a great opportunity to enjoy the new freedom of her sex, to lose her harem veil, to breathe free air as an achieving human creature — but, alas! one's forties are too wise. Pretty as she was, innocent as she was, and eager as her soul was in high emprise of the conflict of world ideals into which she was plunging, we felt that, after all, hidden away deeply in the secret places of her heart, were a man and a home and children.

We whizzed through the dusk in the suburbs of Paris that night, seeing the gathering implements of war coming into the landscape for the first time — the army trucks, the horizon blue of the French uniform, the great training camps, the Red Cross store houses, the scores and scores of hospitals that might be seen in the public buildings with Red Cross flags on them, the munition plants pouring out their streams of women workers in their jumpers and overalls.

The girl porters came through and turned on the lights in the train. No lights outside told us that we were hurrying through a great city. Paris was dark. We went through the underground where there was more light than there was above ground. The streets seemed like tunnels and the tunnels like streets. We came into the dingy station and a score of women porters and red capped girls came for our baggage. They ran the trucks, they moved the express; they took care of the mail, and through them we edged up the stairway into the half-lighted station and looked out into the night — black, lampless, engulfing — and it was Paris!

It was nine o'clock as we stood on the threshold of the station peering into the murk. Not a taxi was in the stand waiting; but from afar we could hear a great honking of auto-horns, that sounded like the night calls of monster birds flitting over the city. The air was vibrant with these wild calls. We were an hour waiting there in the gloom for a conveyance. But when we left the wide square about the station, and came into the streets of Paris, we understood why the auto horns were bellowing so. For the automobiles were running lickety-split through the darkness without lights and the howls of their horns pierced the night. The few street lights burning a low candle power at the intersections of the great boulevards were hooded and cast but a pale glow on the pavements. And as we rode from our station and passed the Tuileries and the Rue de Rivoli, save for the dim outline of the iron railings of the Gardens ten feet from our cab window, we had no sign to mark our way. Yet our cab whizzed along at a twenty-five mile gait, and every few seconds a great blatting devil would honk out of the darkness, and whirl past us, and sometimes we would be abreast of another and the fiendish horns of us would go screaming in chorus as we raced and passed and repassed one another on the broad street. The din was nerve racking — but highly Parisian. One fancied that Paris, being denied its lights, made up its quota of sensation by multiplying its sound!

We went to the Ritz — now smile; the others did! Not that the Ritz is an inferior hotel. We went there because it was really the grandee among Paris hotels. Yet every day we were in Paris when we told people we were at the Ritz, they smiled. The human mind doesn't seem to be able to associate Henry and me with the Ritz without the sense of the eternal fitness of things going wapper-jawed and catawampus. We are that kind of men. Wichita and Emporia are written large and indelibly upon us; and the Ritz, which is the rendezvous of the nobility, merely becomes a background for our rusticity — the spotlight which reveals the everlasting jay in us!

We went to the Ritz largely because it seemed to me that as a leading American orator, Henry should have proper European terminal facilities. And the Ritz looked to me like the proper setting for an international figure.   There, it seemed to me, the rich and the great would congregate to invite him to dinners, and to me, at least, who had imagination, there seemed something rather splendid in fancying the gentry saying, " Ah, yes — Henry J. Allen, of Wichita — the next governor of Kansas, I understand! "   Henry indicated his feeling about the Ritz thus: The night we arrived he failed, for the first time in two weeks, to demand a dress rehearsal in our $17.93 uniforms from 43rd Street in New York. The gold braided uniforms that we saw in the corridors of the Ritz that night made us pause and consider many things.   When we unpacked our valises, there were the little bundles just as they had come from 43rd Street.   Henry tucked his away with a sigh, and just before he went to sleep he called across the widening spaces between sleep and wakening: " I suppose we might have bought that $23.78 outfit, easy enough! "

It was in the morning that the veneer of the Ritz began to wear off for Henry.   He had

pulled a bath and found it cold; they were con-
serving fuel and no hot water was allowed in the
hotels of Paris excepting Friday and Saturday
nights.   The English, who are naturally mean,
declare that the French save seventy-five per cent
of the use of their hot water by putting the two
hot water nights together, as no living Frenchman
ever took a bath two consecutive days.   But it
did not seem that way to Henry and me.   And
anyway we heard these theories later.   But that
morning Henry, who doesn't really mind a cold
bath, was ready for it when he happened to look
around the bathroom and found there wasn't a
scrap of soap.   There he was, as one might say,
au natural, or perhaps better — if one should
include the dripping from his first plunge — one
might say he was au jus!   And what is more, he
was au mad.   He jabbed the bell button that summoned the valet, and when the boy appeared
Henry had his speech ready for him.   " Donnez
mo-i some soap here and be mighty blame toot
sweet about it! "   The valet explained that soap
was not furnished with the room.   It took some
time to get that across in broken French and
English; then Henry, talking very slowly and in
his best oratorical voice, with his foot on the for-
tissimo, cried: " Say!   We are paying," at the

"Donnez moi some soap here and be mighty blame
toot sweet about it!"

dazed look in the valet's face Henry repeated
slower and louder, " We are paying, I say, fif-
teen-dollars — fif-teen dollars a day for these
rooms.   You go ask Mrs. Ritz if she will furnish
soap for twenty?"   And he waved the valet
grandly out.

An hour later we sallied forth to see Paris in
war time.   Our way lay through the lonely Ven-
dome, out by the empty Rue Castiglione, down the
Rue de Rivoli.   So we came into the great beautiful Place de la Concorde; and what a wide and
magnificent waste it was.   Now and then a way-
farer might be seen crossing its splendid distances,
or a taxicab spinning along through the statuesque
grandeur of the place.   But the few moving objects in the white stretch of marble and cement
only accented its lonely aspect.   The circle of
the French provinces was as desolate as the Pom-
peiian Forum, and save for the bright colours
of the banks of flowers that were heaped upon
the monuments to Alsace and Lorraine, the place
might have been an excavation rather than the
heart of a great world metropolis.   Before the
war, to cross the Place de la Concorde and go
into the Champs Elysees was an adventure of a
life time.   One took one's chances.   One sur-
vived, but he had his thrills.   But that morning

we might have walked safely with bowed head and hands clasped behind us through the Place, across the Elysian fields; there we sat for a moment in one of the Babylonian cafés and saw nothing more shocking than the beautiful women of France gathering in the abandoned cafés and music halls to assemble surgical dressings for the French wounded.

In due course, in that first day of our pilgrimage in Europe, we came to the headquarters of the American Red Cross in the Place de la Concorde. The five floors of a building once used for a man's club are now filled with bustling, hustling Americans. Those delicately tinted souls in Europe who are homesick for Broadway may find it in the office of the American Red Cross; but they will find lower Broadway, not the place of the bright lights. The click and clatter of typewriters punctuate the air. Natty stenographers, prim office women, matronly looking heads of departments, and assistants from perhaps the tubercular department, the reconstruction department, the bureau of home relief in Paris, or what not, move briskly through the corridors. In the reception rooms are men from the ends of the earth — Rumanians, Serbians, Armenians, Belgians, Boers, Russians, Japs — every nation

at peace with America has some business sometime in that Paris office of the American Red
Cross.   For there abides the commissioner of the
Red Cross for all Europe.   At that time he was
a spare, well made man in his late thirties,—
Major Grayson M.-P. Murphy; a West Pointer
who left the army fifteen years ago after service
in the Philippines, started " broke " in New York
peddling insurance, and quit business last June
vice-president of the largest trust company in the
world, making the climb at considerable speed, but
without much noise.   He was the quietest man in
Paris.   He was so quiet that he had to have a
muffler cut-out on his own great heart to keep it
from drowning his voice!   There is a soft lisp
in his speech which might fool strangers who
do not know about the steel of his nerves and the
keenness of his eye.   He sat in a roomy office with
a clean desk, toyed with a paper knife and made
quick, sure, accurate decisions in a low hesitant
voice that never backed track nor weakened before a disagreeable situation.   He is the man who
more than anyone else has laid out the spending
of the major part of the first one hundred millions gathered in America by the Red Cross drive
last summer.   He held his rank as Major in the
United States army, and wore his uniform as

though it were his skin, clean, unwrinkled and handsome, with that gorgeous quality of unconscious pride that is, after all, the West Pointer's real grace.

As we sat in that noble room, looking out across the Place de la Concorde, past the Obelisk to the House of Deputies beyond the Seine, it was evident that Henry was thinking hard. The spectacle of Major Murphy's young men in their habiliments of service, Red Cross military uniforms that made them look like lilies of the valley and bright and morning stars, gave us both something to think about. The recollection of those $17.93 uniforms of ours in the rooms at the Ritz was disquieting. We had service hats; these young gods wore brown caps with leather visors and enameled Red Crosses above the leather. We had cotton khaki tunics unadorned, and of a vintage ten years old. They had khaki worsted of a cut to conform to the newest general order. They had Sam Browne belts of high potency, and we had no substitute even for that insignia of power. They had shiny leather puttees. We had tapes. They had brown shoes — we had not given a fleeting thought to shoes. We might as well have had congress gaiters! So when the conversation with Major Murphy turned to a

point where he said that he expected us to go
with him to the French front immediately he
took a look at our Sunday best Emporia and
Wichita civilian clothes and asked casually,
" Have you gentlemen uniforms? " For me
right there the cock crowed three times. Henry
heard it also, and answered slowly, " Well, no —
not exactly."

" Mr. Hoppen," said the Major, " take these
gentlemen down the street and show them where
to get uniforms!" Which Mr. Hoppen went
and did. Now Mr. Hoppen is related to the
Morgans — the J. Pierpont Morgans — and he
has small notion of Emporia and Wichita. So
he took us to a tailorshop after his own heart.
We chose a modest outfit, with no frills. We
ordered one pair of riding breeches each, and one
tunic each, and one American army cap each.
The tunic was to conform to the recent Army
regulation for Red Cross tunics, and the trousers
were to match; Henry looked at me and received
a distress signal, but he ignored it and said non-
chalantly, " When can we have them? " The
tailor told us to call for a fitting in two weeks, but
we were going to the front before that. That
made no difference; and then Henry came to the
real point. " How much," he asked, " will these

be?" The tailor answered in francs and we quickly divided the sum into dollars. It made $100. "For both?" asked Henry hopefully. "For each," answered the tailor firmly. There stood Mr. Hoppen, of Morgans. There also stood Wichita and Emporia. Henry's eyes did not bat; Mr. Hoppen wore a shimmering Sam Browne belt. Looking casually at it Henry asked:

"Shall we require one of those?"

"Gentlemen are all wearing them, sir," answered the tailor.

"How much?" queried Henry.

"Well, you gentlemen are a trifle thick, sir, and we'll have to have them specially made, but I presume we may safely say $14 each, sir!"

Henry did not even look at me, but lifted the wormwood to his lips and quaffed it. "Make two," he answered.

The world should not be unsafe for democracy if Wichita and Emporia could help it!

We went to a show that night with the feeling of guilt and shame one has who has betrayed his family. That $114 with ten more to come for brown shoes, flickered in the spot light and babbled on the lips of the singers. They danced it in the ballet. Each of us was thinking with guilty horror of how he would break the news of that uniform bargain to his wife. So we went home tired that first night, through the grim dark streets of Paris and to our rooms. And there were those 43rd street uniforms still unwrapped in the bureau drawer. Henry again demanded a dress rehearsal. He insisted that as we were going to have to wear them to the front we ought to know how we looked inside of them. But we were weary and again put off the dread hour. The next morning we bought our ten dollar brown shoes, and concluded that there was a vast amount of foolishness connected with this war.

During the long fair days while we waited for Major Murphy to take us to the front, we wandered about Paris, puffing and spluttering through the French language. Henry never was sure of anything but toot sweet and some devilish perversion was forever sticking sophomore German into my mouth, when French should have risen. The German never actually broke out. If it had, we should have been shot as spies. But it was so close that it always seemed to be snooping around ready to jump out. That made it hard for me to shine in French.

These adventures with the French language were not exactly the martial adventures that Charley Chandler, of Wichita, and Warren Finney, of Emporia, thought we would be having at the Front, when they trundled us out to win the war. Yet these adventures were serious. They were adventures in lonesomeness. We could imagine how the American soldier boy would feel and what he would say when this language began to wash about his ears and submerge him in its depths. We could fancy American soldiers wandering through the French villages, unable to buy things, because they couldn't understand the prices. We could understand the dreary, bleak, isolated lives of these American boys, with all the desolation of foreigners hungering always for human companionship, outside of the everlasting camp. And we came to know the misery of homesickness that hides in the phrase, " a stranger in a strange land! "

So we were glad to summon the Eager Soul to dine with us, and we let her order a dinner so complicated that it tasted like a lexicon! We learned much about the Eager Soul that night. She told us of her two college degrees, her year's teaching experience, her four years' nursing, and her people in the old home town. Bit by bit, we picked out her status from the things she dropped inadvertently. And that night in our rooms we assembled the parts of the puzzle thus; one ram-

bling Bedford limestone American castle in the
Country Club district; two cars, with garage to
match; a widowed mother, a lamented father who
made all kinds of money, so naturally some of it
was honest money; two brothers, a married sister; a love for Henry James, and Galsworthy;
substantial familiarity with Ibsen, Hauptman,
Bergsen, Wagner, Puccini, Brahms, Freud,
Tschaikovsky, and Bernard Shaw; a whole-
hearted admiration for Barrie; and a record as or-
ganizer in the suffrage campaign which won in her
state three years ago, plus a habit of buying gloves
by the dozen and candy in five pound boxes! We
could not prove it, but we agreed that she probably bossed her mother and that the brothers'
wives hated her and the sister's husband loved
her to death! She was one of those socially assured persons in the Old Home Town who are
never afraid of themselves out of it! She confessed that she had seen more or less of the
Gilded Youth, before he left for Verdun, and in
a pyrotechnic display of dimples, she admitted
that she had gone to the station to bid the Young
Doctor good-bye. She had been assigned to a
hospital near the Verdun sector, and was going
out the following day. When we left her at the
door of the Hotel Vouillemont, we plunged back

into the encircling gloom of the French language with real regret.

As we went further into the life about us, we felt that all the men were in uniform and all the women in mourning. The French mourn beautifully. France today is the world's tragedy queen whose suffering is all genuine, but all magnificently done. In the shop windows of the Boulevards, and along the Avenue of the Opera are no bright colours — excepting for men's uniforms. In the windows of the millinery shops, purple is the gayest colour — purple and lavender and black prevail. On every street are blind windows of departed shops. Some bear signs notifying customers that they are closed for the duration of the war; others simply stare blankly and piteously at passersby who know the story without words.

Yet if it is not a gay Paris, it is anything but a sad Paris. Rather it is a busy Paris; a Paris that stays indoors and works. For an hour or two after twilight the crowds come out; Sunday also they throng the boulevards. And the theatres are always well filled; and there the bright dress uniforms of the men overcome the sombre gowns of the women and the scenes in lobbies and foyers are not far from brilliant. Bands and orchestras play in the theatres, but the music lacks fire. It is beautiful music, carefully done, artistically executed, but the orchestras are made up for the most part of men past the military age. We heard " La Tosca " one afternoon and in the orchestra sat twenty men with grey hair and the tenor was fat! As the season grew old, we heard " Louise," " Carmen," " Aphrodite," " Butterfly " (in London), and " Aida " (in Milan), and always the musical accompaniment to the social vagaries of these ladies who are no better than they should be, was music from old heads and old hearts. The " other lips and other hearts whose tales of love " should have been told ardently through fiddle and clarinet are toying with the great harp of a thousand strings that plays the dance of death. That is the music the young men are playing in Europe today. But in Paris, busy, drab, absent-minded Paris, the music that should be made from the soul of youth, crying into reeds and strings and brass is an echo, an echo altogether lovely but passionless!

Finally our season of waiting ended. We came home to the Ritz at midnight from a dinner with Major Murphy, where we had been notified that we were to start for the front the next morning. We told him that the new uniforms were

not yet ready and confessed to him that we had
the cheap uniforms; he looked resigned. He had
been entertaining a regular callithumpian parade
of Red Cross commissioners from America, and
he probably felt that he had seen the worst and
that this was just another cross. But when we
reached our rooms that midnight, Henry lifted his
voice, not in pleading, but in command. For we
were to start at seven the next morning, and it
was orders. So each went to his bedroom and
began unwrapping his bundles. In ten minutes
Henry appeared caparisoned like a chocolate di-
vinity! With me there was trouble. Someone
had blundered. The shirt went on easily; the
tunic went on cosily, but the trousers — someone
had shuffled those trousers on me. Even a shoe
spoon and foots-ease wouldn't get them to rise to
their necessary height. Inspection proved that
they were 36; now 36 doesn't do me much good
as a waist line! There is a net deficit of eight
tragic inches, and eight inches short in one waistband is a catastrophe. Yet there we were. It
was half past twelve. In six hours more we must
be on our way to the front — to the great adventure. Uniforms were imperative. And there
was the hiatus! Whereupon Henry rose. He
rang for the valet; no response. He rang for

Eight inches short in one waistband is a catastrophe

the tailor; he was in bed. He rang for the
waiter; he was off duty. There was just one
name left on the call card; so Henry hustled me
into an overcoat and rang for the chambermaid!
And she appeared as innocent of English as we
were of French. It was an awful moment! But
Henry slowly began making gestures and talking
in clear-ly e-nun-ci-a-ted tones. The gestures
were the well-known gestures of his valedictory
to the Republican party at the Chicago Audi-
torium in 1912 — beautiful gestures and impres-
sive. The maid became interested. Then he
took the recalcitrant trousers, placed them gently
but firmly against his friend's heart — or such a
matter, showing how far from the ideal they
came. Then he laid on the bed a brown woollen
shirt, and in the tail of it marked out dramatically
a " V " slice about the shape of an old-fashioned
slice of pumpkin pie — a segment ten or a dozen
inches wide that would require two hands in feed-
ing. Then he pointed from the shirt to the
trousers and then to the ample bosom of his
friend, indicating with emotion that the huge pie-
slice was to go into the rear corsage of the
breeches. It was wonderful to see intelligence
dawn in the face of that chambermaid. The gestures of that Bull Moose speech had touched her

heart.   Suddenly she knew the truth, and it made her free, so she cried, " Wee wee! "   And oratory had again risen to its proper place in our midst! At two o'clock she returned with the pumpkin pie slice from the tail of the brown shirt, neatly, but hardly gaudily inserted into the rear waist line of the riding trousers, and we lay down to pleasant dreams; for we found that by standing stiffly erect, by keeping one's tunic pulled down, and by carefully avoiding a stooping posture, it was possible to conceal the facts of one's double life.   So we went forth with Major Murphy the next morning as care-free as " Eden's garden birds."   We looked like birds, too — scarecrows!

Our business took us to the American Ambulance men who were with the French army. Generally when they were at work they were quartered near a big base hospital; and their work took them from the large hospital to the first aid stations near the front line trenches.   Our way from Paris to these men led across the devastated area of France.   As the chief activity of the French at the time of our visit was in the Verdun sector, we spent most of our first week at the front near Verdun.   And one evening at twilight we walked through the ruined city.   The

Germans had just finished their evening strafe; two hundred big shells had been thrown over from their field guns into the ruins. After the two hundredth shell had dropped it was as safe in Verdun as in Emporia until the next day. For the Germans are methodical in all things, and they spend just so many shells on each enemy point, and no more. The German work of destruction is thorough in Verdun. Not a roof remains intact upon its walls; not a wall remains uncracked; not a soul lives in the town; now and then a sentinel may be met patrolling the wagon road that winds through the streets. This wagon road, by the way, is the object of the German artillery's attention. Upon this road they think the revitalment trains pass up to the front. But the sentinels come and go. The only living inhabitants we saw in the place were two black cats. It must have been a beautiful city before the war — a town of sixty thousand and more. It contained some old and interesting Gothic ecclesiastical buildings — a cloister, a bishop's residence, a school — or what not — that, even crumbled and shattered by the shells, still show in ruins grace and charm and dignity. And battered as these mute stones were, it seemed marvellous that mere stone could translate so delicately the highest groping of men's hearts toward God, their most unutterable longing. And the broken stones of the Gothic ruin, in the freshness and rawness of their ruin, seemed to be bleeding out human aspiration, spilling it footlessly upon the dead earth. And of course all about these ecclesiastical ruins were the ruins of homes, and shops and stores — places just as pitifully appealing in their appalling wreck — where men had lived and loved and striven and failed and risen again and gone on slowly climbing through the weary centuries to the heights of grace toward which the tendrils of their hearts, pictured in the cloister and the apse and the tower, were so blindly groping.   A dust covered chromo on a tottering wall; a little round-about hanging beside a broken bed, a lamp revealed on a table, a work bench deserted, a store smashed and turned to debris and left to petrify as the shell wrecked it — a thousand little details of a life that had gone, the soul vanished from a town, leaving it stark and dead, mere wood and stone and iron — this was the Verdun that we saw in the twilight after the Germans had finished their evening strafe.

From Verdun we hurried through the night, past half a dozen ruined villages to a big base hospital. We came there in the dark before

moonrise, and met our ambulance men — mostly
young college boys joyously flirting with death
under the German guns. They were stationed
in a tent well outside the big hospital building.
They gave us a dinner worth while — onion soup,
thick rare steak with peas and carrots, some sort
of paste — perhaps macaroni or raviolli, a jelly
omelet soused in rum, and served burning blue
blazes, and cheese and coffee — and this from a
camp kitchen from a French cook on five minutes' notice, an hour after the regular dinner.
The ambulance men were under the direct command of a French lieutenant — a Frenchman
of a quiet, gentle, serious type, who welcomed us
beautifully, played host graciously and told us
many interesting things about the work of the
army around him; and told it so simply — yet
withal so sadly, that it impressed his face and
manner upon us long after we had left him.
Three or four times a day we were meeting
French lieutenants who had charge of our ambulance men at the front. But this one was different. He was so gentle and so serious without
being at all solemn. He had been in the war for
three years, and said quite incidentally, that under
the law of averages his time was long past due
and he expected to go soon. It didn't seem to

bother him.   He passed the rum omelet with a
steady hand.   But his serious mien had attracted
the ambulance boys and upon the room of his
office in the big brick hospital they had scrawled
in chalk, " Défense absolutement de rire! "
" It's absolutely forbidden to laugh."   Evidently
American humour got on his nerves.   As we
dined in the tent, the boys outside sang trench
songs, and college songs with trench words, and
gave other demonstrations of their youth.

So we ate and listened to the singing, while
the moon rose, and with it came a fog — more
than a fog — a cloud of heavy mist that hid the
moon.   We moved our baggage from the tent
to a vacant room in a vacant ward in the big hospital.   We saw in the misty moonlight a great
brick structure running around a compound.
The compound was over 200 feet square, and in
the centre of the compound was a big Red Cross
made of canvas, painted red, on a background of
whitewashed stones.   It was 100 feet square.
On each side of the compound a Red Cross blazed
from the roof of the buildings, under the Geneva
lights — lights which the Germans had agreed
should mark our hospitals and protect them from
air raids.

At midnight we left the hospital to visit those
ambulance men who were stationed at the first
aid posts, up near the battle line.   It was an eery
sort of night ride in the ambulance, going without
lights, up the zigzags of the hill to the battle
front of Verdun.   The white clay of the road
was sloppy and the car wobbled and skidded along
and we passed scores of other vehicles going up
and coming down — with not a flicker of light
on any of them.   The Red Cross on our ambulance gave us the right of way over everything
but ammunition trucks, so we sped forward rapidly.   It was revitalment time.   Hundreds of
motor trucks and horsecarts laden with munitions,
food, men and the thousand and one supplies
needed to keep an army going, were making their
nightly trip to the trenches.   When we reached
a point near the top of the long hill, which we
had been climbing, we got out of the ambulance
and found that we were at a first aid dugout just
back of the hill from whose top one could see the
battle.   The first aid post was a cave tunnelled
a few yards into the hillside covered with railroad iron and sandbags.   In the dugout was a
little operating room where the wounded were
bandaged before starting them down the hill in

the ambulance to the hospital, and three doctors and half a dozen stretcher bearers were standing inside out of the misty rain.

As we had been climbing the hill in the ambulance, the roar of the big guns grew louder and louder. We believed it was French cannon. But when we got out of the car we heard an angry whistle and a roar which told us that German shells were coming in near us. As we stood before the dugout shivering in the mist we saw beyond us, over the hill, the glare of the French trench rockets lighting up the clouds above us weirdly, and spreading a sickly glow over the white muddy road before us. On the road skirting the very door of the dugout passed a line of motor trucks and carts — the revitalment train. The mist walled us in. Every few seconds out of the mist came a huge grey truck or a lumbering two-wheeled cart; and then, creaking heavily past the dugout door, plunged into the mist again. Never did the procession stop. At regular intervals the German shells crashed into the woods farther up the hill beyond us. But the silent procession before us — looming out of the mist, passing us, and fading into the mist, kept constantly moving. In the ghostly light of the misty moonshine, the procession seemed to be

spectral — like a line of passing souls.   A doctor
came out of the dugout and started up the hill.
He, too, was swallowed in the mist.   Ahead of
us up the road were noises that told us the Germans were landing bombs there, not half a mile
— perhaps not much more than a quarter of a
mile away.   The stretcher bearers told us that
the Germans were shelling a cross-road.   They
shelled it every night at midnight to smash the
revitalment train.   The shells were landing right
in the road whereon all these trucks and horse
carts were passing.   The doctor who left us returned in a few minutes in an ambulance —
wounded.   Another ambulance came up with
four or five wounded.   A shell had crashed in
and wiped out a truck load of men.   But the procession under the misty moon never stopped —
never even hesitated.   No driver spoke.   No
teams or trucks cluttered up the road.   As fast
as a bomb shattered the road out there behind the
mist, or made debris of a truck, the engineers
hurried up, cleared the way, removed the debris
and the ceaseless procession in the ghostly moonlight moved on.   Another ambulance brought in
two more wounded.

    After one o'clock the bombing stopped.   Some
other cross-road was taking its turn.   Five men

were buried that night in the little cemetery there by the dugout. We stood or sat about for a while! no one had much to say. The grey mist thickened and enveloped us. And we became as very shadows ourselves. Somewhere in the mist up the hill, near where the rocket's red glare flushed on the dim horizon, a man began whistling the intermezzo from " Thais." It fitted the unreality of the scene, and soon two of us were whistling together. He heard me and paused. Then we walked toward one another whistling and met. It was the Gilded Youth from the ship — the Gilded Youth whose many millions had made him shimmer. He was not shimmering there on the sloppy hillside. He was a field service man, and we went back to his machine and sat on it and talked music — music that seemed to be the only reality there in the midst of death, and the spirit that was moving men in the moonlight to forget death for something more real than death. And so it came about that the crescendo of our talk ran thus:

And courage — that thing which the Germans thought was their special gift from Heaven, bred of military discipline, rising out of German kultur — we know now is the commonest heritage of men. It is the divine fire burning in the souls of us that proves the case for democracy. For at base and underneath we are all equals. In crises the rich man, the poor man, the thief, the harlot, the preacher, the teacher, the labourer, the ignorant, the wise, all go to death for something that defies death, something immortal in the human heart. Those truck-drivers, those mule whackers, those common soldiers, that doctor, these college men on the ambulances are brothers tonight in the democracy of courage. Upon that democracy is the hope of the race, for it bespeaks a wider and deeper kinship of men.

So then we knew that under the gilding of the Gilded Youth was fine gold. He was called for a wounded man. As he cranked up his car he asked rather too casually, " Have you seen our friend from the boat — the pretty nurse? " We started to answer; the stretcher bearer called again and in an instant he went buzzing away and we returned to the hospital.

We slept that night in a hospital bed. The week before three thousand men had passed through that hospital — some upon the long journey, so we rose early the next morning. For some way to Henry and me there seemed a curious disquietude about those hospital beds.

In the early morning just after dawn we saw

them taking out the dead from the hospital. The stretcher bearers moved as quickly as they could with their burden through the yard. A dozen soldiers and orderlies were in the hospital compound, but no one turned a head toward the bearers and their burden. There were indeed, in sad deed, "a dearth of woman's nursing and a lack of woman's tears." No one knew who the dead man was. He wore his identification tag about him. No one cared except that it should be registered. If he was an officer he went to one part of the little graveyard just outside the fence; if he was a private he went inside. It was a lonely, heart-breaking sight. And it occurred to Henry and me — we had been among the ghosts on the hill the night before and had slept uneasily with the ghosts in the hospital — that we should give one poor fellow a funeral. So we lined up in the chill dawn, and followed the stretcher bearers and marched after some poor Frenchman to his tomb. It was probably the only funeral that the hospital yard ever had seen, for the soldiers and orderlies and attendants turned and gaped at the wonder, and nurses peered from the windows.

Four days later we were sitting in the courtyard of a little tavern in St. Dizier. A young

French soldier came up, and tried his English on us. He found that we had been to Verdun. And he asked, " Have you heard the news from the big base hospital? " We had not. Then he told us that the night before the German airmen had come to the hospital early in the night and had dropped their eggs — incendiary bombs. An hour later they came and dropped some high explosives. They came again at midnight and because there were no anti-aircraft guns near by — the allies until those August and September German raids never had dreamed that hospitals would be raided — they came again swooping low and turned their machine guns on the doctors and the nurses in the compound who were taking the wounded out of the burning building. Then toward morning they came and dropped handbills which declared, " If you don't want your hospitals bombed, move them back further from the front! "

The Germans were not acting in the heat of passion. They were fighting scientifically, even if barbarously. For every mile a hospital is moved back of the line makes it that much harder to stop gangrene in the wounded. And by checking gangrene we are saving a great majority of our wounded to return to battle.

Nine doctors and fifteen nurses and many wounded were killed that night at Vlaincourt. "And the French officer de liason between the French army and the American ambulance, what of him?" we asked.

"He slept in the hospital and was killed by a bomb," answered the Frenchman.

So our serious faced French lieutenant knew all too well why "It is absolutely forbidden to laugh" in war!

CHAPTER III

THERE is something, though Heaven knows
not much, to be said for war as war. And
the little to be said is said when one declares that
it refreshes life by taking us out of our ruts.
Routine kills men and nations and races; it is stag-
nation. But war shakes up society, puts men into
strange environments, gives them new diversions,
new aims, changed ideals. In the faint breath of
war that came to Henry and me, as we went
about our daily task inspecting hospitals and first
aid posts and ambulance units for the Red Cross,
there was a tremendous whiff of the big change
that must come to lives that really get into war as
soldiers. Even we were for ever pinching ourselves to see if we were dreaming, as we rode
through the strange land, filled with warlike impedimenta, and devoted exclusively to the science
of slaughter. By rights we should have been sitting in our offices in Wichita and Emporia edit-

ing two country newspapers, wrangling mildly
with the pirates of the paper mills to whom our
miserable little forty or fifty carloads of white
paper a year was a trifle, dickering with foreign
advertisers who desired to spread before Wichita
and Emporia the virtues of their chewing gum
or talking machines, or discussing the ever changing Situation with the local statesmen. At five
o'clock Henry should be on his way to the Wichita
golf course to reduce his figure, and the sullen roar
of the muffler cut-out on the family car should be
warning me that we were going to picnic that
night out on the Osage hills in the sunset, where
it would be up to me to eat gluten bread and avoid
sugars, starches and fats to preserve the girlish
lines of my figure.

But instead, here we were puffing up a hill in
France, through underbrush, across shell holes to
a hidden trench choked with telephone cables that
should lead underground to an observation post
where a part of the staff of the French army sat
overlooking the battle of the Champagne. As we
puffed and huffed up the hill, we recalled to each
other that we had been in our offices but a few
weeks before when the Associated Press report
had brought us the news of the Champagne drive
for hill 208. Among other things the report had

declared " a number of French soldiers were ordered into their own barrage, and several were
shot for refusing to go into action thereafter!"
And now here we were looking through a peep-
hole in the camouflage at the battlefield! We
were half way up the hill; below us lay a weedy
piece of bottom land, all kneaded and pock-
marked by shells, stretching away to another
range of hills perhaps five miles, perhaps ten
miles away, as the valley widened or narrowed.
The white clay of the soil erupting under shell
fire glimmered nakedly and indecently through
the weeds.   It was hard to realize that three years
before the valley before us had been one of the
great fertile valleys of France, dotted with little
grey towns with glowing red roofs.   For as we
looked it seemed to be " that ominous tract, which
all agree hides the Dark Tower!"   There it all
lay; the " ragged thistle stalk," with its head
chopped off; " the dock's harsh swart leaves
bruised as to balk all hope of greenness."   " As
for the grass, it grew scantier than hair in lep-
rosy; thin dry leaves pricked the mud, which underneath looked kneaded up with blood!"   It
was the self-same field that Roland crossed!   In
the midst of the waste zigzagged two lines — two
white gashes in the soil, with a scab of horrible

brown rust scratched between them — the French and German trenches and the barbed wire entanglements. At some places the trenches ran close together, a few hundred feet or a few hundred yards marked their distance apart. At other times they backed fearfully away from one another with the gashed, stark, weed-smeared earth gaping between them. We paused to rest in our climb at a little shrine by the wayside. A communication trench slipped deviously up to it, and through this trench were brought the wounded; for the shrine, a dugout in the hillside, had been converted into a first aid station. A doctor and two stretcher bearers and two ambulance men were waiting there. Yet the little shrine, rather than the trenches that crept up to it, dominated the scene and the war seemed far away. Occasionally we heard a distant boom and saw a tall cone of dirt rise in the bottom land among the trenches, and we felt that some poor creature might be in his death agony. But that was remote, too, and Major Murphy of our party climbed to the roof of the dugout and began turning his glasses toward the German lines. Then the trenches about us suddenly grew alive. The Frenchmen were waving their hands and running about excitedly. Major Murphy was a Major — a regular United States Army major in a

One of our party climbed to the roof of the dugout and
began turning his glasses toward the German lines

regular United States army uniform so grand that
compared with our cheap cotton khaki it looked
like a five thousand dollar outfit.   The highest officer near us was a French second-lieutenant, who
had no right to boss a Major!   But something had
to be done.   So the second lieutenant did it.   He
called down the Major; showed him that he was
in direct range of the German guns, and made it
clear that a big six-foot American in uniform
standing silhouetted against the sky-line would
bring down a whole wagon-load of German hardware on our part of the line.   The fact that the
German trenches were two miles away did not
make the situation any less dangerous.   After-
wards we left the shrine and the trenches and
went on up the hill.

The view from the observation trench on the
hill-top, when we finally got there, was a wonderful view, sweeping the whole Champagne battle field.   Hill 208 lay in the distance, still in German hands, and before it, wallowing in the white
earth were a number of English tanks abandoned
by the French.   Lying out there in No Man's
Land between the trenches, the tanks looked to our
Kansas eyes like worn out threshing machines
and spelled more clearly than anything else in the
landscape the extent of the French failure in the

Champagne drive of the spring of 1917. It may be profitable to know just how far the pendulum of war had swung toward failure in France last spring, before America declared war. To begin: The French morale went bad! We heard here in America that France was bled white. The French commission told us how sorely France needed the American war declaration. But to say that the morale of a nation has gone bad means so much. It is always a struggle even in peace, even in prosperity, for the honest, courageous leadership of a nation to keep any Nation honest. But when hope begins to sag, when the forces of disorder and darkness that lie subdued and dormant in every nation, and in every human heart are bidden by evil times to rise — they rise. Leadership fails in its battle against them. For a year after the morale of the French began to come back strong, the French newspapers and French government were busy exposing and punishing the creatures who shamed France in the spring of 1917. German money has been traced to persons high in authority. A network of German spies was uncovered, working with the mistresess of men high in government — the kaiser is not above using the thief and the harlot for his aims; money literally by the cartload was poured into certain departments to hinder the work of the army, and the tragic disaster of the Champagne drive was the result partly of intrigue in Paris in the government, partly of poverty, partly the result of three winters of terrible suffering in the nation, and partly the weakening under the strain of all these things, of this " too too solid flesh and blood." During the winter of 1916–17 soldiers at the front received letters from home telling of starvation and freezing and sickness in their families. And trench conditions in the long hard winter were all but unbearable. When a soldier finally got a leave of absence and started home, he found the railroad system breaking down and he had long waits at junction points with no sleeping quarters, no food, no shelter. French soldiers going home on leave would lie all night and all day out in the open, drenched by the rain and stained by the mud, and would reach home bringing to their families trench vermin and trench fever and trench misery untold, to add to the woe that the winter had brought to the home while the soldier was away. Then when he went back to fight, he found that a bureaucratic clash had left the soldiers without supplies, or food or ammunition in sufficient quantities to supply the battle needs.

In the bureaucratic clash some one lost his head in the army and ordered the men into their own barrage. Hundreds were slaughtered. Thousands were verging on mutiny. A regiment refused to fight, and another threatened to disobey. The American ambulance boys told us that the most horrible task they did was when they hauled eighty poor French boys out to be shot for mutiny! Spies in Paris, working through the mistresses of the department heads, the sad strain of war upon the French economic resources, and the withering hand of winter upon the heart of France had achieved all but a victory for the forces of evil in this earth.

And there we were that summer day, when time and events had changed the face of fate, looking out across the blighted field of Champagne at what might have been the wreck of France.

All is changed now. At every railroad junction the American Red Cross has built cantonments, where beds and food and baths and disinfecting ovens for trench clothes are installed for the homeward bound soldiers of France. The American Red Cross has the name of every French soldier's family that is in need, and that family's needs are being supplied by the American Red Cross. And the sure hope of victory

has given the leadership of France a mastery of
the forces of evil in the lower levels of the Nation's political consciousness that will make it
impossible for the kaiser's friends, the courtesans,
to accomplish anything next winter.

We gazed across the field that afternoon and
seeing the blotched acres, weed blasted, shell-
pocked, blistered with white trenches and scarred
with long jagged barbed-wire rents for miles and
miles, and we thought how perfectly does the
spirit of man mark the picture of his soul's agony
upon his daily work.

It was late in the afternoon when we left that
sector of the line. We passed a bombed hospital
where two doctors and three nurses had been
killed a night or two before. It was a disquieting
sight, and the big Red Cross on the top of the
hospital showed that the German airmen who
dropped the bombs were careful in their aim.
Gradually as we left the Champagne front the
booming guns grew fainter and fainter and finally
we could not hear them, and we came into a wide,
beautiful plain and then turned into the city of
Rheims. It was bombed to death — but not to
ruins. Rheims is what Verdun must have been
during the first year of the war, a phantom city,
desolate, all but uninhabited, broken and battered

and abandoned.   Here and there, living in caves and cellars, a few citizens still stick to their homes.   A few stores remain open and an occasional trickle of commerce flows down the streets. We went to the cathedral and found its outlines there — a veritable Miss Havisham of a ruin, the pale spectre of its former beauty, but proud and — if stone and iron can be conscious — vain of its lost glory.   A gash probably ten feet square has been gouged in the pavement by a German shell, and the hole uncovers a hidden passage to the Cathedral of which no one in this generation knew.   In the hovering twilight we walked about, gazing in a sadness that the broken splendour of the place cast upon us, at the details of the devastation.   The roof, of course, is but a film of wood and iron rent with big holes.   The walls are intact, but cracked and broken and tottering.   The Gothic spires and gargoyles and ornaments are shattered beyond restoration, and the windows are but staring blind eyes where once the soul of the church gazed forth.   Men come and gather the broken bits of glass as art treasures.

That evening at supper in Chalons, we met some American boys who said the French were selling this glass from the windows of Rheims made from old beer-bottles and blue bottles and green bitters bottles, and still later we saw an English Colonel who had bought a job lot of it and found a patent medicine trade mark blown in a piece!

We had been in the place but a few minutes, when we went to the back of the cathedral where we found an excited old man on the sidewalk with a broom in front of a postcard printing office. He spoke to Henry and me, but we could not understand him. He pointed to the stone dust and spawl freshly dropped on the sidewalk and to a hole in the pavement, and then to a broken iron shell. It must have weighed twenty-five pounds. He kept pointing at it, and made it clear we were to touch it. It was still hot! It had dropped in but a few minutes before we came. We went into his shop to stock up on post cards, and as Major Murphy and Mr. Norton, who could talk French, learned that another shell would be due in three or four minutes, we left town.

The road out of Rheims was in full view of the German lines, hidden only, and at that rather poorly, by camouflage — straw woven into mats, and burlap, badly torn. We were between the German guns five miles away, and the sunset. Great holes in the ground beside the road indicated where they had been dropping shells, so our driver tramped on the juice, the machine shot out at fifty miles an hour and we skedaddled.

From the road out of Rheims we dropped into the valley of the Marne, a most beautiful vine-clad valley, where the road turns sharply from the German lines and soon passes out of the German range and the shell holes at the side of the road disappear. But even shell holes would not have taken our eyes from the beauty of that valley as we wound down into it from the hill. Vines were everywhere. Rows and rows of vines, marking a thousand brownish green lines in the earth as far as the eye could see. The grapes were ripe and they gave a tint of purple and brown to the landscape. It glowed with colour. Half a score of little grey, red roofed towns dotted the checkered fields. The sun was slanting through the plain. Tall dark poplars slashed it with sombre greens. As we whizzed through the quaint little villages dashes of colour seemed doused in our faces; soldiers in horizon blue with crimson trimmings and gold on their uniforms, black Moroccans with their gaudy red fezes, flags of staff and line officers fluttering from doors and window sills, all refreshed our eyes with new, strange, gorgeous combinations of colours. And when we passed a town where no soldiers were quartered, there the dooryards were brilliant with phlox and dahlias — even the door yards of those poor wrecked villages deserted after the German bombardment — villages roofless and grey and gaunt and wan, from which the population fled in July, 1914, and from which the Germans themselves a few weeks later were forced to flee, running pell-mell as they scurried before the wrath of the French soldiers.

As we went down into the valley of the Marne where division after division of the French army was quartered upon the population, thousands in a village, where normally hundreds were sheltered, we realized what social chaos must stalk in the train of war. Every few weeks these soldiers go to the front and other soldiers come in. Fathers, husbands, sweethearts of peace times are at the front or dead. The visiting soldiers come " from over the hills and far away," but they are young, and the women are young and beautiful, and they live daily with these women in their houses. Moreover, the emotions of France are tense. Death, doubt, fear and hope lash the home-staying hearts every day. And amid those raw emotions comes the daily and hourly call of the deepest emotion in the human heart. It comes honestly. It comes inevitably.

And then, in a day or an hour, the lover is gone, and new faces appear in the village, in the street, in the home. Five millions of men during the last three years and a half have passed and re-passed, through those fifty miles or so back of the firing line in which soldiers are quartered for rest, where in times of peace less than a million men have lived. And the women are the same honest, earnest, aspiring women that our wives and sisters are, and the men are as chivalrous and gentle and as kind.

For nearly an hour we had been going through these villages crowded with soldiers — kindly French soldiers who were clearly living happily with the people upon whom they were billeted. Then Henry burst forth, " My good Heavens, man — what if this were in Wichita or Emporia! What if your house and mine had ten or twenty fine soldiers in it, and we were away and our wives and daughters were there alone? Thousands and thousands of these young girls flitting about here were just little children three years ago when their daddies left. What if in our streets soldiers were quartered by the hundreds in every block, with nothing in the world to do but rest! What would happen in Wichita and Emporia — or back East in Goshen, New York, or out West in Fresno or Tonapah? What an awful thing — what a hell in the earth, war is!"

And yet we know that young hearts will express themselves as they were meant to express themselves even in the wrack and ruin and waste of war. And this strange picture of love and death sitting together some way reminded us of the phlox and the dahlias blooming in the dreary dooryards of the shattered homes near the battle line. And then our hearts turned to the youth on the boat — that precious load of mounting young blood that came over with us on the *Espagne* where we were the oldest people in the ship's company. And we began talking of the Eager Soul and her Young Doctor and the Gilded Youth. If the war could lash our old hearts as it was lashing them, so that even our emotions were raw and more or less a-quiver in the storm of the mingled passions of the world that overwhelmed us, how much — how fearfully much more must their younger hearts be stirred? How could youth come out of it all unscarred! And she was such a sweet pretty girl, the Eager Soul, so fine and brave and wise — yet her heart was a girl's heart, after all. And the Young Doctor, his keen sensitive face showed how near to the surface was the quick in him. As for the Gilded

Youth, we had seen there on the hill in the misty night the great hammer of the guns pound the dross out of him! And here they were all three alone, in the fury of this awful storm that was testing the stoutest souls in the world, and they were so young and so untried!

The roads over which we had been travelling for two days in our car were military roads. And we could tell instantly when we were inside the thirty kilo limit of the firing line, by looking at the road menders. If they were German prisoners we were outside the thirty kilo strip. For when the Germans discovered last spring that the Allies held more prisoners than the Germans, the Germans demanded a rule for the treatment of prisoners, which should keep them thirty kilos from danger. It was a rule that the Allies had been observing; but the Germans were not observing it, until they found that they might suffer by non-observance. So when we left the German prisoners and came to French road menders — generally French Chinamen or Anamites, or negroes from Dahomey or other oriental peoples, we knew we were soon to come in sound of the big guns. These road menders always were at work. Beside every road a few yards apart, always were little neatly stacked cones of road metal. A road roller always was in sight. No road ever got bumpy and at given distances along the road were repair stations for the government automobiles. Nothing was allowed to stop the machinery of war. At night along these country roads, thirty kilos back from the line we travelled with lights; so that night out of Rheims, we hurried through the night, passed village after village swarming with soldiers, black and yellow and white; for the colour line does not irritate the French; and we saw how gay and happy they were, crowding into picture shows, listening to the regimental band, sitting on the sidewalks before the cafés, or dancing with the girls in the parks. Then a time came when the village streets were lonely and dark and we knew that the bugle had sounded taps. And so in due course we came to the end of the day's journey, at the end of a spur of the railroad, near one sector of the Verdun front. There we found a field hospital of four thousand beds. And when there is to be renewed French activity on the Verdun sector, the first thing that happens is the general evacuation of all the patients in the hospital. It takes a great many railroad trains to clear out a hospital wherein six thousand wounded men are jammed. We saw one hospital train loading.

This hospital had handled twenty-six hundred cases in one day the week before we arrived. The big guns that we had heard booming away for three days as we went up and down the line had been grinding their awful grist. We walked through the hospital, which covered acres of ground. It is a board structure, some of the walls are not even papered, but show the two-by-fours nakedly and the rafters above. Stoves heat most of the wards, and hospital linoleum covers the runways between the rows of beds. Of course, the operating rooms are painted white and kept spotless. The French are marvellous surgeons, and their results in turning men back to the line, both in per cent of men and time are up to the normal average of the war; but they are not so finical about flies and fresh air and unimportant dirt as the English or the Americans. They probably feel that there are more essential things to consider than flies and their trysting places! In this hospital we saw our first wounded German prisoners. We saw boys fifteen years old, whose voices had not changed. We saw men past fifty. We saw slope-shouldered, hollow-chested, pale-faced men of the academic type, wearing glasses an eighth of an inch thick. We saw scrubby looking men who seemed to " be the dirt and the dross, the dust and the scum of the earth."

And we saw also some well-set-up Germans, and in a bull-pen near the railroad station waiting for the trains to take them to the interior of France were six thousand German prisoners — for the most part well-made men. Here and there was a scrub — a boy, a defective, or an old man; showing that the Germans are working these classes through the army; but indicating, so far as one batch of prisoners from one part of the battle line may indicate, that the Germans still have a splendid fighting army. But the old German army that came raging through Belgium and northern France in 1914 is gone. Germany is well past the peak in man power, as shown in the soldiers of the line. It is also likely that the morale of the German line has its best days behind it. The American ambulance men in the Verdun sector told us of a company of German soldiers who had come across a few nights before to surrender, after killing their officers. They appeared at about ten o'clock at night, and told the French to cease firing at exactly that time the next night for ten minutes and another troop of Germans would come across. The French ceased at the agreed hour and thirty more came over and brought the mail to their comrades! That, of course, is not a usual occurrence. But similar instances are found. The best one can say of the German morale in the army is that it is spotted. In civilian life the nearer one gets to Germany the surer one is that the civilian morale seems to be sound. These things we found in the air up near the front line trenches, where German prisoners talk, and where one sees the war " close up."

But we were going still nearer to the German lines, and the next day we set out for Recicourt and arrived there about noon. It is a little bombed village where a few thousand soldiers are quartered, and a few score villagers huddle in cellars and caves by night and go forth to their farms by day. The village lies in a ravine. The railway runs in front of the town, and the week we were there a big naval gun was booming away on the railroad throwing death into the German lines eight or ten miles away. At the back of the town, across a bridge over a brook the white wagon road runs, and that day the road was black with trucks going up to the front line with supplies. We could hear the big guns plainly over in the woods a few miles away. But we had no thought of danger as we tumbled out of

our car. We should have known that bombed
villages don't just grow that way! Something
causes the gaping holes in roofs, the shattered
walls, the blear-eyed windows and battered out-
buildings! Generally it is German shells; but
we had been seeing bombed towns for days, and
we forgot that sooner or later we must meet the
bombs that did the miserable work. As we stood
by the automobiles at Recicourt, kicking the
wrinkles out of our cotton khaki riding breeches
— and mine, alas, had to be kicked carefully to
preserve that pie-slice cut from my shirt tail that
expanded the waistband from 36 to 44 inches —
little did it seem to Henry and me that we should
first meet a German shell face to face in a place
like Recicourt. The name did not sound historic.
But we had scarcely shaken hands around the
group of American Ambulance men who gathered
to greet us before we heard a B-A-N-G! — an
awful sound! It was as if someone suddenly
had picked up the whole Haynes Hardware store
— at Emporia — tinware, farm implements,
stoves, nails and shelf-goods, and had switched it
with an awful whizz through the air and landed
it upon the sheet-iron roof of Wichita's Civic
Forum, which seats six thousand! We looked
at each other in surprise, but each realized that he

must be casual to support the other; so we said
nothing to the Ambulance boys, and they, being
used to such things, let it pass also.   We went on
talking; so did Major Murphy, being a soldier.
So did Mr. Richard Norton, being head of the
American Ambulance Service.   In a minute there
was a fearful whistle — long, piercing, and savage, and then they had taken the Peters Hardware stock in Emporia and dumped it on the
Wichita Union Station.   This time we saw a
great cone-shaped cloud of dirt rise not 400 feet
away — over by the wagon road, across the brook
from us.   Still no one mentioned the matter.   It
seemed to Henry and me to be anything but a
secret, but if the others had that notion of it,
far be it from us to blab!   An ambulance driver
came lazying around the corner and began to start
his car.

"Any one hurt, Singer?" asked a handsome
youth named Hughes, of the Corps.

"Man hit by the first shell up here by the railroad.   I'm going after him."

"Hurt badly?" asked another boy.

"Oh, arm or shoulder or something blown off.
I'll be back for lunch."

The details interested us; we could see that the
secret was being uncovered.   Again came an

awful roar and another terrific bang — this time
the dust cloud rose nearer to us than before —
perhaps 300 feet away. Every one ducked. In
five seconds they had taught me to duck. It's
curious how quickly the adult mind acquires useful information. But Henry for some reason
got a bad start, and his duck needed correction.
To duck, you scrooch down, and shrink in, to get
as much as possible of your body under the eaves
of your steel helmet. Somewhere between the
second and third bang, they got a helmet on me.
No one knows where it came from, nor how it
got there. But there it was, while they were cor-
recting Henry's duck. In spite of them, when he
ducked, Henry would lean forward, thus multiplying his exposure by ten. But it really does a
fat man little good to duck anyway; the eaves of
his helmet hardly cover his collar. It was while
they were trying to telescope Henry that some
one grabbed me by the arm and said:

"Come on! Let's go to the abri!"

Abri was a brand new word to me, but it
seemed to be some place to go and that was
enough for me.

"Where" (read this line with feeling and em-
phasis) "is the abri?" The ambulance boy took
me by the arm and led me on a trot to a dugout

covered with railroad iron, and logs and sand bags, and we went in there and found it full of French officers. They have some sense. The abri would not turn a direct explosion of a shell; but it would shield one against a glancing blow and against the shrapnel which sprays itself out from the point where the shell hits like a molten iron fountain. After the ninth bomb had come over we left the abri. The Germans had been allowancing Recicourt to nine a day. But that day they gave us three more prunes for dessert. They came very close and fairly fast together. As they came Henry was sitting in the barn where the ambulance boys had their meals. Lunch was on the table and Henry was writing. The shells sounded just outside the barn. "What are you writing, Mr. Allen?" asked Major Murphy. "I'm sketching," stuttered the Wichita statesman, "a sort of a draft of the American terms of peace!"

After three extra bombs had come in the Germans turned their guns from the town, and we had our lunch at our ease. And such a lunch! A melon to begin with; a yellow melon that looks like the old-fashioned American muskmelon and tastes like a nectar of the gods, followed by onion soup. Then followed an entrée, a large thin slice

"Come on! Let's go to the abri!"

of cold sausage which they afterward told us was
made of horse meat, a paté of some kind, then
roast veal sliced thin and slightly underdone with
browned potatoes; then new beans served as a
separate course; then fruit and cheese and coffee
and cigars!   And that in a barn!

We had to go up to a first aid station after
lunch so we piled into an ambulance, were but-
toned in from the back by the driver, and went
sailing up the hill and into the woods.   They
told us that we were in the Avecourt Woods in
the Forest of Hess.   We remembered that but a
few weeks before when we were in our newspaper
offices, that the Avecourt Woods had been the
scene of some fierce and bloody fighting.   And
as we rode up the hill we heard the French cannon roaring all about us.   We were told that
four thousand cannon were planted in the Avecourt Woods, but only about a thousand of them
were active that day.   Yet we could see none, so
completely were they hidden by camouflage.
The woods were barren of leaves or branches
though they should have been in foliage.   We
gazed through the windows of the ambulance into
the stark forest with its top off, and then rather
gradually it occurred to me that the white objects carefully corded against the tree trunks were

not sticks of cord wood at all, as they seemed, and
as they should have been if the wood had been
under the ax instead of under fire. They were
French seventy-five shells — deadly brass car-
tridges two feet long, all nicely and peacefully
corded against the trunks of the big trees! We
rode through them for several miles. Beside the
road always were the little heaps of road metal,
little heaps of stone, and always the engineers
stood ready to refill the holes that might be made
by the incoming shells. And occasionally they
were coming in; though they seemed to be landing in a distant part of the forest. The ear be-
comes curiously quick at telling the difference between what are known as arrives and departs.
The departs were going out that day at the ratio
of 32 to one arrive. For the Germans had wasted
enough ammunition on the Verdun sector and
were trying to economize! Still the arrives were
landing in the Avecourt wood every minute or
so, and they were disquieting. Only the chirping
of our own broad-mouthed canaries there in the
roofless forest gave us cheer. For some way the
sound of the shells of our own guns shrieking
over us is a deep comfort; it is something like
the consolation of a great faith.

At last, seven or eight miles in the forest, we

came upon the first aid post, a quarter of a mile from the opposite edge of the wood and but half a mile from the front line trenches of Verdun. The first aid post there was a cellar, half exca- vated, and half covered with earth, and roofed with iron rails, logs and sandbags. The usual French doctors, stretcher bearers and American Ambulance men were there. And there was the little cemetery, always found at a first aid post where those are buried who die on the stretchers or in the dugout. It was lovingly adorned by the French with the tri-colour of France, with bronze wreaths, with woodland flowers, and was alto- gether bright and beautiful in the bare woods. They showed us a shell by the cave — a gas shell that had come over during the morning and had hit on the oblique and had not exploded. It was gently leaking chlorine gas, which we sniffed — but gingerly. Other shells were popping into the place and fairly near us with some regularity and enthusiasm, and it seemed to Henry and me that we had no desire to stare grim war's wrinkled front out of countenance, and we hoped that the Major and Mr. Norton were nearly ready to go back. But we heard this:

From the Major: "How far forward can we go toward Hill 304; we would like to see it, but have no desire to go further than you care to have us."

And from the French lieutenant in charge: " Go to Berlin if you want to!"

It occurred to Henry and me, considering our feelings, that the Major's nonchalant use of that " we " was without the consent of the governed. But when he started forward we followed. Our moral cowardice overwhelmed our physical cowardice, and our legs tracked ahead while our hearts tracked back. The Major swung along the road at a fast clip; Mr. Norton went with him. For short-geared men we followed as fast as we could, but it was at a respectful distance. Nearer and nearer we came to the open field, and by the same token, quicker and nearer and hotter came the German shells. We were continually on the duck. Our progress had an accordion rhythm that made distance come slow. We came to a dead mule in the road. He had been bombed recently, and was not ready for visitors. Now a mule is not nature's masterpiece at his best; but in the transition state between a mule and hamburger, a mule leaves much to be desired. As we passed the forward reaches of the mule, Henry began his kidding. He always begins to guy a situation under emotion. " Bill," he cried, " if

we die we'll at least save our nice new hundred
dollar uniforms down there in Paris!" And
from me he got this: " And say, Henry — if
we die we won't have to face our wives and tell
'em we paid that much for a two-piece suit!
There's that comfort in sudden death!"

It seemed to Henry and me that we had seen
all there was to be seen of the war. Hill 304
would be there after the treaty of peace was
signed and the Major and Norton then could
come to see it. But they were bound for Berlin;
so we slowly edged by that poor mule; he seemed
to be the longest mule we had ever — well, he
seemed to be a sort of trans-continental mule, but
we finally got past him and came to the edge of
the woods. It took about three ducks to twenty
yards, and passing the mule we had four downs
and no gain. That gave the Germans the ball.
So when we got to the edge of the wood and
were standing looking into the French trenches
and at Hill 304 off at our right, after the Major
had handed Norton the field glasses and Norton
had considerately handed them to Henry, who
passed them to me for such fleeting glance as po-
liteness might require, the Germans came back
with that ball. It came right out of Berlin, too.
One could hear it howl as it crossed the Thier-

garten and went over Wilhelm Strasse and
scream as it whizzed over Bavaria.   There never
was another such shell.   And we ducked —
all of us.   Henry said he never saw me make
such a duck — it was the duck of a life-time.
And then that shell landed.   It was a wholesale
hardware store that hit — no retail affair.   The
sound was awful.   And then something inside of
me or outside tore with an awful rip.   We had
been reading Dr. Crile's book on the anesthesia
of fear, and suddenly it occurred to me that the
shell had hit me and torn a hole in me and that
fear had deadened the pain.   Slowly and in terror my right hand groped back to the place of the
wound, expecting every moment to encounter
blood and ragged flesh.   We were still crouched
over, waiting for the fountain of junk to cease
spraying.   Nearer and nearer came the shrink-
ing fingers to the wound.   They felt no blood,
but something more terrible!   There, dangling
by its apex, hung that pie-shaped slice of shirt
from those cotton khaki trousers — ripped clear
out!   And Paris fifty miles away!

Slowly we unfolded ourselves from the duck.
And as we came up — sping! went a sharp me-
tallic click on Norton's helmet.   A bit of shrapnel had hit it.   Under a hat he would have been

killed! So we went back to the first aid post —
me holding those khaki trousers up by sheer force
of will, and both hands!

So long as Norton and the Major had led the
way from the dugout, it simultaneously flashed
over Henry and me that we should lead the way
back, and not leave all the exertion to our com-
panions. So we set the pace back.

At the first aid post we stopped for breath.
The French welcomed us back, and we rested a
moment under their hospitality. Our own
French guns were carolling away; the arrives
were coming in. It seemed to Henry and me
that we were not so badly frightened as we knew
we were. For we kept a running fire going of
airy persiflage — which was like the noise of
boys whistling through a graveyard. Henry
said: " That German gunner is playing by ear!
His time is bad, or else it's syncopated." Then
to Major Murphy: " Nice sightly location that
Hill 304; but I noticed real estate going up a
good deal in the neighbourhood!" And to the
assembled company in the dugout he remarked
as he pulled out his pipe, a short Hiram Johnson,
bulldog model that he had bought on the Rue de
Rivoli, " If you gentlemen will get out your gas
masks now I'll light my dreadnaught!" Which

he did and calmed his iron nerves. So in a few moments we came out of the post and went to our ambulance which would take us back to Recicourt. Clouds had blown across the sky and as we passed the gay little cemetery by the dugout, we were shocked to see the body of a French lieutenant laid ready for burial. He had met death while we played the fool in our twenty minutes' walk.

We rode to Recicourt greatly sobered, and it was hours before we could get back our spirit. Of course, eventually, kind hands pinned up the rent in the corsage of those khaki trousers. They used a dozen big steel safety pins as large as railway spikes. And that night as we were preparing for bed in a shack near a hospital, Henry gazed curiously at the job as it glittered before him in our corner, when, his friend's tunic being removed, the wealth of metal was uncovered. Henry was impressed. " Bill," he said gently, as he gazed admiringly at his friend's armour, " I don't know as I ever saw a man before with so much open plumbing on him as you're wearing these days ! "

For a long time we lay awake and talked about the day's experience, and particularly our half day under fire. We agreed that really it was not so bad. We were scared — badly scared ; but we

So we went back—me holding those khaki trousers
up by sheer force of will and both hands!

could laugh at it, even at the hottest of it, and it was never so exceedingly hot. Yet we might have been killed. Thousands who died, went out in just such mild places as we had been through, and probably went out laughing as we might have gone, by a jiggle of a quarter of an inch one way or another of the German's gun. Our Wichita and Emporia soldiers, we said, would doubtless live days and weeks under what we had seen and would grow fat on it. Then Henry mused: " I wonder if that young French lieutenant there in the woods went out smiling! " And then for a long time no one spoke, and at last we slept.

CHAPTER IV

WHEREIN WE FIND THAT "OUR FLAG IS STILL THERE"

THIS chapter will contain the story of our visit to General Pershing and the American troops. But before we came to that part of France which holds our men we passed through divers warlike and sentimental enterprises which lay across our path, and while we relate the story of these adventures, the reader must wait a few moments before we disclose the American flag. But the promise of its coming may buoy him up while the preliminary episodes clog the narrative.

One afternoon we were chugging along in our Red Cross ambulance coming down from the first aid posts where we had been talking to some American Ambulance boys on the French Front, when we noticed the arrives were landing regularly so we knew that the Germans were after something in the neighbourhood — perhaps a big gun, perhaps an ammunition dump. We were speculating upon the nature of the target when we whirled around a corner and saw it. It was a cross-road. Four roads forked there; the Germans, of course, had it marked. It was getting its afternoon pour parler; for they believed that the ammunition trains would be passing that cross-road at that time. And as we looked out of the windows of the ambulance our hearts jumped — at least Henry's and mine jumped — as we saw that between us and the forks of the road a great French camion had skidded and stalled, with two wheels over the embankment that raised the road from the swamp about us, effectually blocking our way. " This," said Major Murphy, taking in the situation quickly, " is a mighty dangerous place." As the word " place " escaped him he was on the ground. He had slid through a window of the ambulance. The ambulance drivers — Singer and Hughes — neglecting to unlock the ambulance doors, ran up the road and began working with the drivers of the camion to get the great van on the road again. The other occupants of the ambulance also hurried to the camion — through the windows of the ambulance; no one was left to unbutton the thing for Henry and me. Henry insists that he was there alone; that he was afraid to follow me through the window for fear of sticking in it. He had not been avoiding fats, sugars and starches for a year and had no girlish lines in his figure. And the arrives were certainly bouncing in rather brashly. The rest of us were out in the open where we could duck and perhaps avoid the spray of shrapnel. But an ambulance was no more protection against fifty pounds of German junk than an umbrella. And there sat Henry in the ambulance wistfully looking through the window of the vehicle and realizing that his exposure was less in a dignified sitting posture in the ambulance than it would be horizontally half in and half out of the thing, held fast in the vain endeavour to get away. So he waited for the next " arrive " to come with commendable fortitude. And then it came. It sounded like the old granddaddy of all shells. We fancied we could sense its direction; possibly that was imagination. But anyway we looked toward the German lines and realized Henry's grave danger. And then it struck — whanged with an awful roar about seventy-five feet from us, against the bare trunk of a shell-stripped tree. We knew without looking that the shell had hit the tree. Then our consciousness recorded the fact that a French soldier had been standing by that tree. And slowly and in terror we turned our eyes tree-ward. The tree was a mass of splinters. It looked like a special sale of toothpicks in a show window. Then we turned our eyes toward the place where we had last seen the French soldier. We hardly dared to look. But instead of seeing a splatter of blood and flesh upon the earth by the tree stump, we saw the soldier rise from the buck-brush where he had been ducking, and light a cigarette. The shell had hit not a dozen feet above him, but had sprayed its fountain from him, instead of toward him. He had some trouble lighting his cigarette and was irritated for a second at his inconvenience. But so far as we could see, the fact that death had reached for him and missed him by inches had left no impression upon his mind. Three years in war had wrought some deep change in him. Was it entirely in his nerves or was it deeper than nerves, a certain calmness of soul — or was it merely a dramatic expression of a soldierly attitude? We did not know. But to Henry and me, who had been rescued from death by that tree that stopped the shell headed straight for us, it seemed that we should come back after the war was over and nail a medal of honour and a war cross on the stump, and put up a statue there with an all-day program! We had no desire to hide our fright! It relieved us to chatter about the tablet on that tree stump! ·

The French soldier strolled over to us; helped to straighten out the camion, and when we learned that he was going down the hill we gave him a lift. He was a hairy, dirty, forsaken looking poilu who, washed and shaved and classified, turned out to be an exchange professor from the Sorbonne, who had spent a year at Harvard, and it was he who told us of the bombing of the hospital at Landrecourt; we'll call it Landrecourt to fool the censor, who thinks there is no hospital there. At the mention of the hospital the Major turned to us and said: "That's where we sent that pretty red-headed nurse who came over with you on the boat. And," added the Major, "that is the hospital equipped by Mrs. Chesman, of New York!" whose name is also changed to fool the censor. It was a better known name!

"Say," exclaimed Henry, "the Aunt of the Gilded Youth!"

"You mean our ambulance boy who came over on the boat with you — the multimillionaire?" asked the head of the American Ambulance service.

"The same," answered Henry, who turned to

He had some trouble lighting his cigarette and was
irritated for a second at his inconvenience

me and said in his oratorical voice: " The plot thickens." Then the Frenchman told us the story of the raid: How the airmen had come at midnight, dropped their bombs, killing nurses and doctors, and how the discipline of the hospital did not even flutter. He said that the head nurse summoned all her nurses, marched them to the abri at the rear of the hospital, and stood at the door of the abri, while the girls filed in, and just as the last nurse was going into the dugout with the head nurse standing outside, the airmen dropped a bomb upon her and erased her! None of the nurses inside was hurt. Two doctors were killed and a number of patients. Landrecourt was on our way and we hurried to it.

Was there ever a martial adventure without a love story in it? Little did it seem to Henry and me as we left our humble homes in Wichita and Emporia to make the world safe for democracy, that we two thick-set, sedentary, new world replicas of Don Quixote and Sancho Panza should be the chaperons and custodians of a love affair. We were not equipped for it. We were travelling light, and our wives were three or four thousand miles away. No middle-aged married man gets on well with a love affair who is out of daily reach of his wife. For when he gets into the barbed wire tangle of a love affair, he needs the wise counsel of a middle-aged woman. But here we were, two fat old babes in the woods and here came the Gilded Youth, the Eager Soul and the Young Doctor — sping! like a German shell — right into our midst, as it were.

There at Landrecourt we found the Eager Soul, a badly scared young person — but tremendously plucky! And mad — say, that girl was doing a strafing job that would have made the kaiser blush! And the fine part of it was, that its expression was entirely in repression. There was no laugh in her face, no joy in her heart, and we scarcely knew the sombre, effective, business-like young person who greeted us. And then across the court we saw something else that interested us. For there, walking with his patrician aunt, we saw the Gilded Youth. Evidently he had heard of the raid, had run over from Valaincourt on some sort of military permission.

"Oh, yes," answered the Eager Soul to our enquiring eyes. "Mrs. Chesman — this is practically her hospital. I mean she and her group are keeping it equipped and going — a wonderful work. I mean here is a real thing for a woman to do. And, oh, the need of it!"

"Nice sort?" This from Henry, observing

" Oh, yes," answered the Eager Soul to our enquiring
eyes. " Mrs. Chessman — this is practically her
hospital "

that there was no move toward us, on the part of the Gilded Youth and Auntie. Henry may have had his theory for their splendid isolation. But it received no stimulus when the Eager Soul answered:

" Oh, yes, I believe so. I haven't met her yet. They all say she is charming." Henry looked at me. She caught the glance. Then to cover his tracks he grinned and said: " Charm seems to run in their family."

" Yes," she returned amiably. " One meets so many nice people on the boat."

And Henry, still in pursuit of useful social information, insisted: " Well, are they as nice in the war zone as they are — on the boat? "

We got our first dimple then, and the Eager Soul tucked in a wisp of red hair, as she answered:

" Well, really, I've been too busy to know." She turned absent-mindedly toward the figure of the Gilded Youth, across the court. But the dimples and the smile faded and she closed the door firmly and finally on romance, when she said: " On the record of service shown by my entrance card, they have made me assistant to the new head nurse who is coming over from Souilly tonight."

After we had told her that we were going to American headquarters soon, she smiled again, to show us that she knew that when we went probably we would see the Young Doctor. But she let the smile stand as her only response to Henry's suggestion of a message. In another moment she turned to her work.

"Well," said Henry, "some pride! 'One meets so many nice people on the boat!' The idea being that her outfit at home is just as good as Auntie's group in New York, even if he didn't introduce her! You know I rather like the social spunk of our Great Middle West!"

While we were talking the Gilded Youth began moving Auntie slowly but rather directly around the court to us. It occurred to me that perhaps he realized that we were the only social godfathers that the Eager Soul had in Europe, and that if he introduced us to Auntie it would be an indication that the affair of the boat, if it was an affair, was to be put upon a social basis! And in two minutes more he had docked Auntie at our pier. A large, brusk, well-groomed, good-looking woman of fifty was Auntie. Her Winthrop and Endicott blood advertised itself in her Bostonese, but she was sound and strong and the way she instantly got at the invoice price of

Henry and his real worth, pleased me. She was genuine American. The thing that troubled me was the fear that Henry would begin too soon to lambast onion soup. But he didn't and in a few moments we were having this dialogue:

HENRY: " Oh, yes, indeed; we've grown fond of her. Her father was —"

AUNTIE: " Oh, yes, I knew her father. Mr. Chesman and he were interested together in New Mexican mining claims in the eighties; I believe they made some money. But —"

THE GILDED YOUTH: " Well, Auntie — would you mind telling me how —? "

AUNTIE: " Why, on her application blank, of course, with her father's name, age and residence."

THE GILDED ONE: " But you never mentioned it to me? "

AUNTIE: " Nor to her, either. Why should I? This is hardly the place to organize the Colonial Dames! I believe you said a few minutes ago that you had met her on the boat."

HENRY: " One meets so many nice people on the boat! "

ME: " You've heard of the woman who said she didn't know the man socially, she had just met him coming over on the boat! "

The Gilded Youth looked quickly at me, catching me suppressing a wink at Henry, who grinned at the expiring ghost of it. Then Auntie led the talk to the raid of the night before; and invited us to come up for a night's sleep in a civilized bed in the hospital. We were quartered for the night with the Ambulance boys, sleeping in a barn loft, so naturally, we accepted her invitation. Just as we were leaving to get our baggage, out into the court came the Eager Soul bearing a letter. We did not see the address, but it was, alas, plainly dimpled in her face, for the Gilded Youth to see, and after greeting him only pleasantly, she handed the letter to us, saying: " Would you be good enough to deliver this for me at Gonrecourt next week, as you are passing? It is to a friend I met on the boat! "

" Yes," said Henry; " one meets so many nice people on the boat."

" Sometimes," she answered, as she turned to her work.

That night we slept like logs until after midnight; then the moon rose, and the hospital began to come to life. The stir and murmur of the place wakened us. And we realized what a moonlight night means in a hospital near the front line. It means terror. No one slept after moon-

rise. It was a new experience for Henry and me.
So we rose and met it. And we realized that
in scores of hospitals all over the war zone, on
the side of the allies, similar scenes were enact-
ing. The Germans were literally tearing the
nerves out of hundreds of nurses by their raiding campaign — nurses whom the raiders did not
visit, but who were threatened by every moonlight night!

It must have been after two in the morning,
when we saw the Eager Soul and the Gilded
Youth walking around the court as they used to
pace the deck together. Once or twice they
passed our window, and we heard their voices.
They were having some sort of a tall talk on philosophical matters, which annoyed Henry. The
ocean and onion soup and philosophical theorizing
never seemed reasonable, normal expressions of
anything properly in the cosmos to Henry; he
professed to believe that persons who tolerated
these things would sooner or later be caught
using the words " group " and " reaction " and
" hypothesis," and he would have none of them.
But for all that she used the word group and
once confessed that she was a subscriber to the
New Republic, Henry did like the Eager Soul;
so he waked me up from a doze to say: " Bill,

she's putting him through the eye of the needle all right.   And he's sliding through slick as goose-grease.   I heard him telling her a minute ago that the war isn't for boundaries and geography; but for a restatement of human creeds.   Then she said that steam and electricity have over-capitalized the world; that we are paying too highly for superintendence and that the price of super-intendence must come down, and wages must come up.   Then he said that he and his class will go in the fires burning out there — melted like wax.   And she told him that they both had a lot of stolen goods on them — bodies and minds, and hearts cultivated at the expense of their fellow creatures whose lives had been narrowed that theirs might be broadened.   And you should have heard her talk about the Young Doctor — a self-made man, who had earned his way through college and medical school, and made his own place professionally.   She said he was the Herald of the New Day.   " Bill," sighed Henry, " what would you give if you could talk like that — again? "   But from me, drowsily, came this: " Henry — do you suppose she will get around to that slapping tonight she promised him on the boat?   That would be worth staying up to see! "

" She'll never slap him. He'll never need it. She's talked him clear out of the mood! "

" Yes, she has — yes, she has," came from me. And Henry insisted:

" She may have to slap the Doctor; but she has steered this boy out of the danger zone into the open sea of friendship."

" Oh, yes, she has; oh, yes, she has," came the echo from the other bed! And Henry subsided.

But the buzzing about the hospital would not let us sleep. At three o'clock evidently they were serving tea to the nurses, or lunch of some kind. The moon was shining straight down into the court; the Gilded Youth and the Eager Soul had gone in, and another couple, a stenographer and a hospital orderly were using it as a parlour.

" Queer, queer business, this love-making under the rustle of the wings of death," said Henry. A French plane flying across had filled the compound for a moment. But everyone soon recognized its peculiar buzz. Then for a few seconds from afar came the low ominous hum of the German planes. But they circled away from us. Perhaps the French drove them back. However, it was the excitement in the court that caused Henry's remark. For the young people did not deflect their monotonous course about the compound, when the sky-gazers had returned indoors. Around and around they went, talking, talking, talking, with the low insistent murmur of deeply interested people. Their nerves were taut; emotion was raw; they were young, and their blood moved riotously. And there was the moon, the moon that, since man could turn his face upward, has been the symbol of the thing called love. And now all over that long line slashed across the face of Europe, the moon is the herald of death. Men see it rise in terror, for they know that the season of the moon is the season of slaughter. Yet there they walked in the hospital yard, two unknown lovers, who were true to the moon.

Henry's next remark was: " Bill, fancy when you were young doing your courting out there where a shell is liable to wipe you out any second. We at least had the advantage of elm trees to protect us from the shafts of death."

" Do you suppose, Henry," answered his friend, " that they miss the drip of oars, the shade of the overhanging willows, the suggestive whisper of waters frisking over the ripples at the ford? How can they make love in such a place? "

" ' Gold,' " replied Henry, quoting from Solomon, who was wise, " ' is where you find it! ' " Then we heard the insistence of the lovers' babble drawing near us again. As they turned a corner, Henry heaved a sigh at the perversity of youth in the flaunting neglect of sleep and death, which ever are vital to middle years. We both looked out to the white courtyard, heard the snarl of another plane, obviously French, but still disconcerting, saw the slow even pace of the lovers, unaffected by the approaching growl of the plane, and it came to me to quote one wiser even than Solomon: " O death, where is thy sting! "

We took but a cat-nap that night, and in the morning set down the score on our love affair. The record indicates that during the day Henry had lost; during the night he had won. He put it down in his black book against the time when we should get to Paris, where money would buy things. For we ate at camps, slept in hospitals or in barns or in mess rooms of the ambulance men, and day by day and night after night we saw much misery and were " acquainted with grief." There are so many kinds of hospitals in France! The great streams of broken men that flow unceasingly down from the front are divided as they reach the base hospitals and field hospitals into scores of smaller currents, each flowing to a separate place, where specialists treat the various cases. The blind go one way; those dumb with shell-shock go another; jaw cases separate from men with scalp wounds, and hip fractures are divided from shoulder fractures as the sheep from the goats. Travelling about among the hospitals one picks up curious unrelated and unexplained bits of information; as, for instance, that the British Tommy is the most patient man in Europe under pain. He likes to distinguish between himself and his wound and is likely to reply to the doctor any fine morning, " Me? Oh, I'm right at the top form, Sir; but my leg is bothering me a bit, Sir!" The Canadian isn't so game under a roof as he is under the open sky and in the charge. And the American grunts more than he should. But here is a queer thing. The French tubercular soldier is despondent. With Americans, tuberculosis breeds hope. Perhaps it is the buoyancy of the young blood of our country; but no American feels he is ever going to die with tuberculosis. He feels he is hit hard; that it may take six months or a year to get on his feet; after that — he goes on dreaming his dream. But the tubercular French soldiers are the saddest looking men in Europe.

Back in Kansas last spring we had heard a story to the effect that the Germans were inoculating the French and Belgians behind the lines of the allies with tubercular bacteria. We asked French and American and British doctors about that story, and they all answered that there was nothing to it. The doctors told us that the Germans have a cheaper and better way to fill France with tuberculosis than by wasting serum on their enemies. And then, one day in a tuberculosis hospital we picked up this story, which explained what the doctors meant.

We met a young man from Lille. It was his birthday; Henry bought him a bouquet. He told us his story. He said:

" Three years ago when the war broke out I was 19 years old and was living in Lille with my parents. The Germans came to our house one day with their guns and took me away. They took me to a town in Germany; I think it was Essen, where they made me work in an iron or steel mill. I worked fourteen hours a day, slept on straw outside the works in a shed, had only the clothes they took me in and had only bran to eat!"

" Only bran? " we asked, doubting it.

" Only bran," the interpreter repeated, and from half a dozen cots near by, where others who had suffered as he had, heard our question, came the echo of his confirmation, " Only bran to eat!" He soon caught cold, and soon the " cold " became tuberculosis, and after three years of this his sick days exceeded his work days, and in due course he and five hundred others were assembled, put on a train and shipped out of Germany through Switzerland to Evian in France. Three hundred thousand of these poor husks, men, women, and children, have been dumped into France in the last seven months. Two trainloads of them arrive at Evian every day. The men and women, mostly tubercular, do not tarry. They push on into France, a deadly white stream.

In time the week ended that marked our first trip to the French front. During that week we lived almost entirely in the war zone, and under war conditions. The food was good — better than good, it was excellent, but not plentiful, and the beds were clean and full of sleep. The only physical discomfort we found was in the lack of drinking water. We were warned against all local water.

My feelings on the subject of the French coffee and milk were something like Henry's antipathy to onion soup. But we both loved water with our meals. We had been vaccinated against typhoid, and we were rather insistent that we could drink any kind of water, if it was reasonably clean. But men said " this country is no place to drink water. It has been a battle-ground and a cemetery for three years." Still we insisted, and then, Mr. Norton, head of the American ambulance, told us this one: " Out behind a barrage once near the Champagne; helping the stretcher bearers; nasty weather, rain, and cold. But there we were. We couldn't get in. We ducked from shell hole to shell hole. Finally I found a nice deep one, with water in the bottom — oh, maybe five feet of water in a fifteen foot hole, and I stayed there; two days and nights. My canteen went dry, and for a day or two I scooped water out of the shell hole and drank it. Good enough tasting water so far as that goes, and fresh too! But at the end of the third day, I decided it wasn't agreeing with me and quit."

" Why?" we asked. " Did you leave the shell hole?"

" No — oh, no. It was a good shell hole. I

stayed. But you know Fritzie came up!" he answered.

So our taste for water with our meals, which is America's choicest privilege, passed. Henry could drink the coffee, but it didn't taste good to me. The brackish red wine they served with the army ration tasted like diluted vinegar and looked like pokeberry ink. It seemed only good to put in our fountain pens. A tablespoonful would last me all day. Our week's trip ended at Monter-en-Der, where there was a hotel and an Ambulance corps unit that had been over to visit the American troops and had brought back from the commissary department much loot. Among other things was water — bottled water, pure unfermented water. And when we sat at table they brought me a bottle.

Try going seven days on pokeberry ink and boiled coffee yourself and note the reaction. Your veins will be dry; your stomach will crackle as it grinds the food. The water in that bottle, a quart bottle, evaporated. They brought another. It disappeared. They brought a third. The waiters in the hotel were attracted by the sight. No Frenchman ever drinks water with his meals, and the spectacle of this American sousing himself with water while he ate was a

rare sight. The waiters gathered in the corner
to watch me. Henry saw them, and motioned
toward me, and tapped his forehead. They went
and brought other waiters and men from the bar.
He was a rare bird; this American going on a
big drunk on water. So they peered in doors,
through windows and stood in the diningroom
corners to watch the fourth bottle go down. And
when at the end of the meal the American rose,
and walked through the crowd, they made way
for him. A desperate man at least commands
respect, whatever his delusion may be.

And that night we left the French front, and
nosed our car toward Paris.

There we made preparations to go to the headquarters of the American Army. In Paris also
we got into our new regulation Red Cross uniforms. Ever since man first pinned a buffalo
tail to the back of his belt, and stuck a rooster
feather in his matted hair, he has been proud of
his uniform. Sex vanity expresses itself most
gorgeously in a uniform, and when they put
Henry and me into uniforms, even carefully re-
pressed Red Cross uniforms, open at the neck
and with blue dabs on our coat lapels to distinguish us from the " first class fighting man," we
were so proud that often five or six consecutive

minutes passed when we weren't afraid of what
our wives would say about the $124 each had
spent for the togs. At times our attitude toward
our wives was not unlike that of drunken rabbits
hunting brazenly for the dogs! But when we
slipped into citizen clothes, sobriety and remorse
covered us, and we shook sad heads. We wore
the uniforms little about Paris; for our Sam
Browne belts kept us returning salutes until our
arms hurt. They couldn't break me of the habit
of saluting with a newspaper or a package or a
pencil in my hand. And my return of the interminable round of salutes from French, British,
and Italian soldiers who throng Paris, probably
insulted — all unbeknownst to me — hundreds of
our allies, and made them sneer at our flag. So
it seemed best for us to wear these uniforms only
where soldiers congregated who would know us
for the gawks that we were and forgive us our
military trespasses. Then a real day came when
our Red Cross duties took us to General Pershing's headquarters.

For Americans during the year 1918, " Somewhere in France," will mean the Joan of Arc
country. It is not in the war zone, but lies among
the hills of Central France, a four or five hours'
auto ride from Paris. To reach the American

He was a rare bird; this American going on a big
drunk on water

" Somewhere in France " from Paris, one crosses the battle-field of the Marne, and we passed it the day after the third anniversary, when all the hundreds of roadside graves that marked the French advance were a-bloom and a-flutter with the tricolour. Great doings were afoot the day before on that battle-field. Bands had played triumphant songs, and orators had spoken and the leaders of France — soldier and civilian — had come out and wept and France had released her emotions and was better for it. We passed through Meaux and hurried on east to St. Dizier, where we stopped for the night. We put up at a dingy little inn, filled to overflowing with as curious a company as ever gathered under one roof. Of course there were French soldiers — scores of them, mostly officers in full dress, going to the line or coming from it. Then there were fathers and mothers of soldiers and sisters and sweethearts of soldiers and wives of soldiers bound for the front or coming home. And there we were, the only Americans in the house, with just enough French to order " des oeufs " and coffee " au lait " and " ros bif and jambon and pain " and to ask how much and then make them say it slowly and stick the sum up on their fingers. We were having engine trouble. And our

car was groaning and coughing and muttering in
the gloomy little court of the inn.   Around the
court ran the sleeping rooms, and under one end,
forty feet from the diningroom, was what was
once the stable, and what now is the garage.
Frenchmen wandered up, looked at our chauffeur
(from Utica, N. Y.) tried to diagnose the
case, found we did not understand and then
moved away.   But it was a twelve-cylinder American machine and the Frenchmen, discovering
that, kept coming back to it.   As we sat on the
cement platform of the tavern, kicking our heels
against it and bemoaning the follies of youth
which had corrupted our Freshman and Sophomore French, there came and sat beside us a
pretty woman.   She had black snappy eyes, fresh
dark skin, and jet black hair, so curly that it was
almost frowsy.   She listened to us for a moment, then hopped aboard our talk like a boy
flipping a street car: " Kansas — eh?   I once
lived in Oklahoma City.   My father ran the Bee
Hive!"

"Angels of mercy, angels of light!"   This
from me.   "Say, will you interpret for us?"

"Sure mike! sir," she said.   And then added:
"And if it's engine trouble my husband upstairs
is a chauffeur.   Shall I get him?"   And when

she returned with him, he fell to, glad enough to
get a look into a twelve-cylinder American car.
Henry stood by him, and with the woman acting
as interlocutor, between our driver and her husband we soon had the trouble located and the
dissimulator — Henry maintains that all engine
trouble is connected in some way with a dissimulator — rectified, and while the job was going on,
he expounded the twelve cylinders to the French,
puffed on his dreadnaught pipe, and left the lady
from Oklahoma City to me. She was keen for
talk. Between her official communiqués to her
husband and our driver, she got in this:

"Yes, I know Frank Wickoff in Oklahoma
City — knew him when he was poor as Job's turkey, and then my folks used to borrow money
at his bank. Before we came to Oklahoma City
we lived in Austin. We ran the Good Luck, or
was it the Fair; no, we ran the Fair in Dallas."
At a quick look at her face from me she laughed
and said: "Oh, yes, I'm Jew all right. No," she
returned to a query, "I never was in Wichita.
But when we moved to Blackwell we used to take
the *Beacon!*"

"Henry, come here," came the call from me.
"Here is old Subscriber and Constant Reader!"
Then Henry came up and the subsequent proceed-

ings interested me no more. For Henry took the witness. And the three of us, kicking our heels on the cement wall below us, sat swapping yarns about mutual friends in the Southwest. It seems that in France the lady is a pedlar who goes from town to town on market day with notions and runs a little notion wagon through the country between times. She told us of an air raid of the night before on St. Dizier where eleven people had been killed and urged us to stay for the funeral the next day. It was to be a sight worth seeing. Most of the dead were women and children. There was nothing military in the little town but the two hotels that housed soldiers and their friends and relatives going to the front and coming back. Yet the Germans had come, dropped a score of bombs on the town, then had flown away for another town, dropping their hateful eggs across country as they went. Luneville had lost half a dozen, Fismes half a score, and other towns of the neighbourhood, accordingly — all civilians, mostly women and children; and not a town raided had any military works or if it had a munition factory, the bombs had hit miles from the plants.

We were beginning to realize slowly what a hell of torture and disease and suffering this war

Henry puffed on his dreadnaught pipe and left the
lady from Oklahoma City to me

means to France. Half a million tuberculars in
her homes, spreading poison there; two million
homeless refugees quartered beyond the war
zone; millions of soldiers living in the homes fifty
miles back from the line, every month bringing
new men to these homes left by their comrades
returning to the battle front; air raids by night
slaying women and babies; commerce choked with
the offering to the war god; soldiers filling the
highways; food, clothing and munitions taking
all the space upon the railroads; fuel almost pro-
hibitively high; food scarce; and always talk of
the war — of nothing, absolutely nothing but the
war and its horrors. That France has held
so long under this curse proves the miracle
of her divine courage! As we sat under the
shrouded torches in the inn courtyard and considered what life really means to the men and
women of St. Dizier, once more we wondered
how we at home would react under the terrific
punishment which these people are taking; what
would Wichita do with her houses bombed, her
homes crowded with refugees; her parks and
schools and public buildings turned into barracks,
her stores filled with gaping empty shelves, her
railroad yards clogged with munitions, and ever
the mourners going about the street and man to

his long home. How would Emporia act with the pestilence that stalketh in darkness for ever near her; with her women and children slaughtered, merely to break the morale of the people and cause them to plead for peace; with cripples from the war hidden away in a hundred sad homes, with fatherless children and children born out of wedlock among the things that one had to face daily? Perhaps our young Jewish friend thought we were wearying of her. For she rose and said, " Well, good-night, gents — pleasant dreams! "

Pleasant dreams — indeed!

But in the morning we arose refreshed and hurried along a misty plain, forty miles or so from the American troops. Always in the background were great bushy trees, and lush green grass, and the thing was composed. How the French manage to compose their landscape is too much for me. But at any of a thousand points the scene might have been photographed for a Corot, by getting a few good-looking girls in nighties to dance on the grass of the middle distance! American landscape has to be picked apart to have its picture taken; a tree selected here, a hill there, a brook yonder, and if ladies in nighties are needed, they are brought from afar! They are not indigenous to the soil. But one feels that in France they might come sidling out from behind any willow clump with their toes rouged ready for the dance!

The road that morning seemed traversing a great picture gallery, unwinding into life as from a dream within a dream! And then, after two hours of joyous landscape, we waked and saw America! Now America was not a vision; it was substantial, if not beautiful. As we switched around a bend in the road we came upon America full-sized and blood raw — a farmer boy — bronzed, milk-eyed, good-natured, with the Middle West written all over him. He wore a service hat at a forward pitch over his eyes; in his hands, conched to tremulo the sound, he held an harmonica; his eyes were aslit in the ecstasy of his own music; from the crook of his arm dangled a bridle, and he sat cross-legged high up on the quarter deck of a great four-story, full-rigged Missouri mule. He didn't salute us but called " Hi " as we passed, and then we knew that " our flag was still there " and that we were near our troops.

The boys must be popular in the neighbourhood. For in the next village, which by the way was a town of ten thousand, our American Red

Cross uniforms were treated with distinguished courtesy. Henry wanted a match. He could talk no French but a little boy at the inn, seeing him fumbling through his clothes with an unlighted pipe, came running to us with a little blue box of matches. Henry gave the boy a franc — more to be amiable than anything else. The boy flashed home to his mother proud as Punch! And just as we were pulling out of the village the boy came running to us with another little blue box of matches. We thought the boy had discovered that matches would bring a franc a box from Americans and was preparing to make his fortune. So Henry took the box, and as the car was moving handed the boy another franc. We noticed him waving his hands and shaking his head. And when we were a mile out of the village Henry opened his second box and found his original franc in it. The boy's mother was ashamed that he should have taken any money for a box of matches, and had made him bring back the money with another box to show how much the French appreciate the Americans coming to France. We met many instances like that.

Soon the road was cluttered up with American soldiers. They were driving motors, whacking mules, stringing along the by-paths and sweating

And he sat cross legged

copiously under the autumn sun. We wondered in passing what an American farmer boy and his self-respecting mule thought of the two-wheeled French carts they were using. Then we turned the corner and came into a new view; we saw our first troop of American soldiers quartered in a French village. They were busy building barracks. We stopped and visited them, and they showed us their quarters: In barns, in lofts of houses, in cellars, in vacant stores — everywhere that human beings could slip in, the American soldiers had installed themselves. The Y. M. C. A. hut was finished, and in it a score of boys were writing letters, playing rag-time on the pianos, and jollying the handsome, wise-looking American women at the counter across one end of the room. An Irish Catholic padre in a major's uniform was in charge of the sports of the camp and he literally permeated the Y. M. C. A. hut. He was the leader of the men. The little village where this troop lived faded into the plain and we rode again for five miles or so, and then came to another and another and still another. At that time thirteen villages in an arc of forty miles or so contained most of our American troops. We stopped many times on our long day's journey. Once we stopped for mid-day

dinner and there came to Henry and me our first
estrangement.   It is curious, as the poet sings,
" how light a thing may move dissension between hearts that love — hearts that the world in
vain has tried and sorrow but more closely tied."
Well — the thing that came between us was cooking — cooking that has parted more soul mates
than any other one thing in the world!   For two
weeks more or less we had been eating in the
French mess, or eating at country hotels or country homes in France, eating good French country
cooking, and it was excellent.   A mid-day meal
typically was a melon, or a clear soup, or onion
soup, brown and strong; a small bit of rare steak
or chop, or a thin sliced roast in the juice with
browned potatoes or carrots, a vegetable entrée —
peas, spinach, served dry and minced, or string
beans; then raw fruit, and cheese.   The bread, of
course, was black war bread, but crusty and fine.
That was my idea of a lunch for the gods.   What
we got at the American mess was this: a thick,
frowsy, greasy soup — a kind of larded dish-
water; thin steak fried hard as nails, boiled beans
with fried bacon laid on the beans — not pork and
beans, but called pork and beans — with the beans
slithery and hard and underdone; lettuce, cabbage, and onions soused in vinegar, white bread

cut an inch thick, soft and spongy, boiled potatoes that had stood in the water after they were
cooked done, and then bread pudding, made by
pouring water on bread, sticking in some raisins,
stirring in an egg, and serving a floury syrup
over it for sauce! There was enough, of course,
to keep soul and body together. But the cooking
had spoiled a lot of mighty good food. And
Henry liked it! There were two preachers with
us, and they bragged about the " good old American cooking! " And when they heard me roar
they said, " He is insulting the star-spangled ban-
ner," and Henry threatened to take my pajamas
out of his black valise!

After passing through many villages crowded
with our troops we came to the headquarters of
the American Expeditionary forces. We found
General Pershing in a long brick building — two
or three stories high, facing a wide white parade
ground. The place had been used evidently as a
barracks for French soldiers in peace times, and
was fitted to the uses of our army. We met a
member of his staff, a sort of outer guard, and
with scarcely a preliminary halt were taken to
the general. He seems easy of access, which is
a sign that he plays no favourites and has no
court. Anyone with business can see him. He

met us in a plain bare room with a square new American-looking desk in the midst of it. He sat behind the desk, cordial enough but with the air of one who will be pleased to have business start, and politenesses stop. So we plunged straight to the business in hand. We were from the American Red Cross in Paris, and our leader had come to get a definite idea of what part the Red Cross was to play in the recreation activities of the army. The Y. M. C. A. was spending millions upon recreation problems. The Red Cross had millions to spend.

Recreation in Paris, of course, means soldier hostels, homes, clubs, houses where American soldiers can go while in Paris on leave of absence. The Red Cross had one single donation of one million dollars to be devoted to a club for American soldiers in Paris. The Y. M. C. A. had started to equip two or three great Parisian hotels as clubs. The Red Cross had money donated for certain other recreation purposes in camp. The Y. M. C. A. believed it should control the camp and Parisian recreation activities of the American troops.

We stated our case about as briefly as it is here written, and in three minutes. In two minutes more General Pershing had assured us that there

would be no need to spend money for hotels or
clubs in Paris, that few soldiers would be given
leave to go to Paris, and that the lavish expendi-
ture of American money in Paris would be bad
for America's standing in France.

And then he allotted the recreation problems
of men in the hospitals to the Red Cross, and the
recreation enterprises for men outside of hospitals to the Y. M. C. A.

He was brief, exact, candid and final. He
stood for the most part, as he talked; spoke low,
fumbled for no word, and looked into his hearers'
eyes. The politician looks over their shoulders.
We spoke for two or three minutes with him
about the work of our troops this winter, and
were impressed with the decision of the man.
He seemed — perhaps subconsciously — afraid
that public opinion at home would demand that
he put our men into the trenches to hold their own
sector too early. He evidently believed that during our first winter the men should go in by squads
and perhaps companies or later in regimental
units for educational purposes, working with the
English and the French learning the trench game.
But we felt clearly that he believed strongly that
it would be spring before we should occupy any
portion of the line ourselves. There was a firm-

ness about him, not expressed in words. No one could say that he had said what we thought he had conveyed to us. Yet each of us was sure that the General would not be moved from his decision. He breathes confidence in him into people's hearts. He never seems confidential; though he is entirely candid. Again one feels sure that there is no court around him. He seems wise with his own wisdom, which is constantly in touch with the wisdom of every one who may have business with him. He will not be knocked off his feet; he will do no military stunts. The American soldiers will not go into action until we have enough troops to hold our part of the line and we will not start an offensive until we can back it up. This all came glowing out of the firm, kind, wise, soldierly face of General Pershing, and it needed no words to verify it. Superfluous words might have contradicted the message of his mien; for they might have added boast to simple statement.

It is all so orderly, so organized, so American, this thing we are doing in France. It is like the effective manipulation of a great trust. The leadership of the American forces in France in the army and in the Red Cross and the Y. M. C. A. is made up of men known all over the

United States; the names of those leaders who
are soldiers may not be mentioned. They have
dropped out of American civilian life so quietly
that they are scarcely missed. Yet for weeks we
lived in the hotel with one of the prominent figures in American finance who is working eighteen hours a day buying supplies, assembling war
material — food, fuel, clothing — putting up
scores of miles of barracks, building a railroad
from tidewater to the American headquarters,
equipping it with American engines, freight cars,
and passenger coaches; sinking piles for the first
time in a harbour which has been occupied for
two thousand years, and unloading great ships
there which were supposed to be too big for that
port. He is the marvel of the French. Hundreds like him are over there lending a hand.
They are about to handle in a year an army half
as large as the other allies have been three years
building. Houses, furniture, fuel, food, guns,
ammunition, clothing, transportation, communication, medicine, surgeons, recreation — the
whole routine of life for a million men and more
must be provided in advance by these organizing
men. This work, so far as these men consider it,
is purely altruistic. They are sacrificing comforts at home, money-making opportunities at

home, and they are working practically for nothing, paying their own expenses, and under the censor's wise rules these men can have not even the empty husks of passing fame. For their names may not be mentioned in the news of what the Americans are doing in Europe. Yet wherever one goes in Europe he is running across these first-class men. Their sincerity and patriotism may not be questioned.

But they are getting something real out of it all. The renewal of youth in their faces through unstinted giving is beautiful to see. They are going into a new adventure — a high and splendid adventure, and while many of them may snap back after the war to the old egoistic individualistic way of looking at life, their examples will persist, and their lives, when they go back to the old rut, will never be the same lives that they were before.

But here is a story, an American story which has in it the makings of a hero tale. It came to us in Paris, bit by bit. We saw it and no one told it to us. Yet here it is, and it should begin in form. Once upon a time in America when the people were changing their gods, a certain major god of finance named James Hazen Hyde, head of a great insurance company, fell into disfavour; and the people, changing their gods, cast him away. If men had been serving the old gods they would have said, " Go it while you're young," to the youth, but instead they said unpleasant things. So he went to France and vanished from the map, but he did not entirely understand why he was banished. He had done nothing that other young gods did not do and he was amazed, but he faded. He lived in Paris as an exile, not as a god, and he couldn't for the life of him tell why. But when the war came he had a mighty human desire to serve his country; just to serve, mind you, not to be exalted. He was fifty years old, too old to pack a rifle; too old to mount an airship; too old to stop a bullet without taking two or three other good men and true, younger than he, to watch him. So he had hard work to find service. Then along came the American Red Cross and it wanted servants — not major generals, not even captains; but just chauffeurs and interpreters and errand boys and things. And young Jimmy Hyde, who had been the Prince of Wales of the younger gods of fashionable finance, and who was cast out when the people changed their gods, came to Red Cross headquarters with his two cars, and offered them and himself to serve. And they put him in a uniform, with a Sam Browne belt, and a Red Cross on his cap; and it was after all his country's uniform, and he was a servant of his country. And men say that even in the days of his young godhood he was not so happy, nor did his face shine in such pride as it shines today. For he is a man. He serves.

After our visit to the American troops we went down to Domremy, the birth place of Joan of Arc. It was good to view her from the aspect of her Old Home Town. There is a church, restored, where she worshipped, and the home where she was born and lived. It was a better house than one is led to suppose she lived in, and indicates that her people were rather of more consequence than common. We visited the home, went into the church, and walked in the garden where she met the angel; but we met postcard vendors instead. Yet it is a fair garden, back from the road, half hidden by a wall, and in it is a lovely drooping tree. A fair place it was indeed for an angel to choose. Some way Joan leaves me without much enthusiasm. Perhaps it is because she has had two good friends who have done her bad turns. The Pope, who made her a saint, and Mark Twain, who made her human. It is difficult to say, off-hand, which did her the worse service. Some way, it seems to me, she could live in our hearts more beautifully in the remote and noble company of myths like the lesser gods, made by men to express their deepest yearnings for the beautiful in life. The pleasant land in which she lived, the gentle hills whereon she watched her flocks, and the tender sky of France, all made me happy, and if Joan did not get to me, perhaps it was because one can take away from a place only what he brings there.

When we left Domremy, the mills — soft green hills, high but never rugged, stretched away in the misty purple distance and we dropped into those vales where Joan watched her sheep and heard the voices. It did not seem impossible, nor even difficult to hear voices amid such beauty. So we fell to discussing the voices that reach this world. And Henry said: " Always there are voices in this earth — always they come in youth, calling us forward and upward. And if we follow them, though they lead to long marches and hard bivouacs, and to humiliation and sorrow, yet are we happy and triumphant."

" But Germany? " insisted someone. " Where were her voices? "

" Her voices came when Heine sang, and Bee-

thoven made music, and Goethe and Schiller
wrote and Schopenhauer thought! If ever a land
had the philosophy and the poetry of democracy
Germany had it. Democracy tried to bloom in
the revolutionary days of the forties, but Germany strangled her voices. And now —"

" And now there are no voices in the world!"
sighed one of our party; but even as he spoke
from out of the purple distance came the thin
faint sound of a bugle trembling among the hills.
It was an American bugle. And Henry caught
its significance, and cried: " There is the new
voice — the voice that the world must follow if
we find the old peace again on earth."

CHAPTER V

IN WHICH WE DISCERN THINGS "BY THE DAWN'S EARLY LIGHT"

A T the close of one fair autumn day our car developed tire trouble, in a village " Somewhere in France," not far from the headquarters of the American Army. There are four excellent reasons for deleting the name of the town. First, the censor might not like to have it printed; second, because the name of the place has escaped my memory; third, because there is a munition factory there and it should not be mentioned, and fourth, because even if the name of the place returned to me, its spelling would get lost in transit. In passing it should be said in this connection that it seemed to Henry and me that the one thing France really needed was a pronounceable language and phonetic spelling. The village where we stopped really was not a village in the Kansas sense; it was twice as big as Emporia and nearly half as big as Wichita, which is

70,000. But the thing that made the place seem like a village to us was the town crier. As we sat in the car he came down the street beating a snare drum and crying the official news of the sugar ration; he was telling the people where they could get sugar, how much they should pay for it and how much they should use for each member of a family a month.

" Why," asked Henry of an English speaking bystander, " don't you put that in your daily newspaper; why keep up the old custom? "

" We have no daily newspaper," answered the inhabitant.

" All right, then, is there any reason why the news won't wait for the weekly? " asked Henry.

" And we have no weekly and no monthly and no annual. We have no newspaper in this town."

That stumped us both. In America every town of five thousand has its daily newspaper, and frequently two dailies, and in the West every town of five hundred people has its weekly newspaper. With us the newspaper crystallizes public sentiment, promotes local pride, and tries to be the social and intellectual centre of the community. A community of twenty-five thousand without a newspaper — and we found that this community

As we sat in the car he came down the street beating
a snare drum and crying official news of the
sugar ration

never had supported a newspaper — was unthink-
able to us in terms of any civilization that we
knew.   How do they know about the births,
deaths, and marriages, we asked; and they told
us that the churches recorded those things.   How
do they know about the scandal?   And we remembered that scandal was older than the press;
it was the father of the press, as the devil is the
father of lies.   How do they know how to vote?
And they told us that newspapers hindered rather
than helped that function.   How did they record
local history?   And in our hearts, we knew who
had recorded so much local history, that most of
it is not worth recording and that tradition takes
care of what is left.   But how did they manage
to create a town spirit, to vote the bonds for the
city waterworks, to establish the public library,
to enforce the laws, to organize the Chamber of
Commerce, to get up subscriptions for this, that
or the other public benevolence?   And men shook
their heads and said: Water has run down hill
many years; perhaps it will keep on running, even
without a newspaper.

It was a sad blow to Henry and me, who
thought our calling was a torch-bearer of civilization.   Indeed, one may digress and say that we
found the whole estate of the press in France

rather disenchanting. For advertising is not regarded as entirely " ethical " in France. The big
stores sometimes do not advertise at all; because
people look with the same suspicion on advertising drygoods and clothing merchants as we in
America look upon advertising lawyers and doctors. So newspapers too often have to sell their
editorial opinions, and the press has small influence in France, compared with the influence of
the press in what we call the Anglo-Saxon countries.

But in that French village of twenty-five thousand people without a newspaper we found a
civilization that compared favourably with the
civilization in any American town. While the
tire was going on it developed that a cog had
slipped in the transgression of the car — or something of the sort, so we were laid up for an hour,
and we piled out of our seats and took in the
town. We found four good bookstores there —
rather larger than our bookstores at home. We
found two or three big co-operative stores largely
patronized by industrial workers and farmers, and
they were better stores by half than any co-operative stores we had seen in America. For with us
the co-operative store is generally a sad failure.
Our farmers talk big about co-operation, but they

sneak around and patronize the stores that offer
the best bargains, and our industrial workers
haven't begun to realize how co-operative buying
will help them. We found no big stores, in the
American sense, but we found many bright, well-
kept shops. In electrical supplies we found the
show windows up to the American average, which
is high indeed; but in plumbing there was a sag.
We discovered that the town had comparatively
few sewers. The big, white-tiled bathroom with
its carload of modern fixtures which adorns the
show window of at least one plumber's shop in
every American town — we missed. The bath-
tub is not a household need in France. Yet some
way we surmised that if our towns could have
better bookstores and fewer bathtubs we might
have felt easier in our minds for the palladiums
of our liberties. And it can't be laid to the picture shows — this slump in the American book
reading average; for the French towns are just
as full of picture shows as American towns.
That superiority in bookstores which lies with
the French over the Americans, should give us
pause. It more than overbalances our superiority
in country newspapers. And then as we walked
about the town that evening in the sunset ponder-
ing upon these things we came to the town park.

It was not a large park; but it lay close down to the main street —"right in the heart of the city," we would say at home. Everyone in town who moved about, to the stores from the residential streets, had to pass through that park. In it were certain long rows of grey-barked trees — trees with trunks that shimmered like the trunks of sycamores, but that rose sheer from the ground forty feet before branching, and then spread widely and calmly into mighty sprays of foliage. One could not walk under those trees day after day and year after year through life and not feel their spell upon his heart. "From the old grey trunks that mingled their mighty boughs high in the heaven," to those whose lives lay underneath, in busy and perhaps more or less sordid routine, must inevitably come "the thought of boundless power and inaccessible majesty!" And that is a good thought to keep in the heart. That grove in the midst of that little French town was worth more to it than sewers, more than a daily newspaper, more than a trolley line or a convention hall. For it called incessantly to men a mute inexorable summons to the things outside ourselves that make for righteousness in this earth. We in America, we in the everlasting Wichitas and Emporias, are prone to feel that we can make

for righteousness what or when we will by calling an election, by holding a public meeting, by
getting a president, a secretary and a committee
on ways and means, by voting the bonds! But
they who walk daily through groves like this,
must in very spite of themselves give some
thought to the hand that "reared these venerable columns and that thatched the verdant
roof!" Now in every French town, we did not
find a grove like this. But in every French town
we did find something to take its place, a historic spot marked with a beautiful stone or
bronze; a gently flowing river, whose beauty was
sacredly guarded; a group of old, old buildings
that recalled the past, a cathedral that had grown
almost like the woods themselves, out of the visions of men into the dreams of men. And these
dumb teachers of men have put into the soul of
France a fine and exquisite spirit. It rose at the
Marne and made a miracle.

And ever since the Marne that spirit has ruled
France. Essentially it is altruistic. Men are not
living for themselves. They are living for something outside themselves; beyond themselves,
even beyond the objects of their personal affec-
tion. Men are living and dying today not for
any immediate hope of gain for their friends or

families, but for that organized political unit which is a spiritual thing called France. We Americans who go to France are agreed that we have never in our lives seen anything like the French in this season of their anguish. They are treading the winepress as no other modern nation has trodden it, pressing their hearts' blood into the bitter wine of war. They grumble, of course, as they do their hard stint. The French proverbially are a nation of grumblers. Napoleon took them grumbling for fifteen years to glory. He took them grumbling to Moscow, and brought them grumbling back. They grumbled under the Second Empire and into the Republic. In 1916 they all but grumbled themselves into revolution. One heard revolt whispered in a thousand places. But they did not revolt. They will not revolt. Grumbling is a mere outer mannerism. In their hearts they are brave.

Over and over again as we went about France were we impressed with the courage and the tenacity of the French. By very contrast with their eternal grumbling did these traits seem to loom large and definite and certain. We met Dorothy Canfield in Paris, one of the best of the younger American novelists. She told us a most illuminating story. She has been two years in

France working with the blind, and later super-
intending the commissary department of a training camp for men in the American Field Ambulance service. She is a shrewd and wise ob-
server, with a real sense of humour, and Heaven
knows a sense of humour is necessary if one gets
the truth out of the veneer of tragedy that sur-
faces the situation.[1] It seems that she was riding
into Paris from her training camp recently, and
being tired went to sleep in her compartment, in
which were two civilians, too old for military
service. She was awakened by a wrangle and
then — but let her tell it:

"Then I saw a couple of poilus sticking their
heads in our window shaking a beret and asking
for contributions to help them enjoy their week's
leave of absence in Paris. My two elderly
Frenchmen had given a little, under protest, saying (what was perfectly true) that it would go
for drink and wouldn't do the poilus any good.
And one of the soldiers was declaiming about the
fat bourgeois who stayed at home and let himself be defended and then wouldn't give a helping hand to the poor soldier on rest leave! To
get rid of them, I put a franc in the beret. This

[1] This story appeared in *Everybody's Magazine* in
Dorothy Canfield's own words.

was received with acclamations, and they inquired to whom should they drink a toast with
the money. I said, 'Oh, give a good Vive
l'Amerique. That'll suit me best!' They both
shouted, 'Oh, is Madame an American?' And
to the dismay of the two bourgeois, put first one
long leg and then another through the window
and came in noisily to sit down (they were standing on the running-board all this time with the
train going forty miles an hour . . . a thing
which was simply unheard-of in France before
the war . . . one of the 'privileges' which the
poilu take!). Well, they shook hands with me
two or three times over and assured me they had
never seen an American before . . . and indeed
the two bourgeois looked at me curiously. Then
one of them began to talk boisterously, express-
ing himself with great fluency and occasionally
with a liberty of phrase which wasn't conventional
at all, another poilu privilege! They sat down,
evidently for a long visit. They were typical
specimens: one was noisy, fluent, slangy, coarse,
quite eloquent at times, a real Parisian of the
lower classes, the kind which leaves its shirt open
at the neck over a hairy chest and calls itself
proudly 'the proletariat.' The other was a fresh-
faced, vigorous country man from Bourgogne,

They were standing on the running board all this time
with the train going forty miles an hour

the type that corresponds to the middle western American, a kind of Emporian! He hadn't much to say, but when he did speak, spoke to the purpose. They both, through all their roughness and coarseness and evident excitement over starting on their 'permission,' had that French instinctive social tact and amenity (of a sort) which keeps decent women from being afraid of them or from hesitating to talk with them; and they were both very sincere, and desperately trying to express something of the strange confusion that is in everybody's mind ever since the war . . . what are we all doing anyhow!

" Here are some of the things the fluent Paris ' cockney ' said . . . for the type corresponds in Paris to the lower-class cockney of London.

" ' See here, you know, we've had enough of it . . . *we can't stand it any more!* I'm just back from the Chemin des Dames . . . you know what that's been for the last month ' . . . then he gave me a terrible description of that battle . . . ' how do you *expect* men to go back to that . . . do you know what happens to you when you live for twenty–thirty days like that? . . . you go mad! Yes, *that's* what happens to you . . . that's what's the trouble with me now . . . I know I sound wild. I am wild . . . *I can't*

stand any more . . . it's more than flesh and
blood can endure to go back into that! Why
don't the Americans *get* in it if they are going
to? Oh, yes, I know they can't any sooner . . .
but why didn't they get *in,* before! Oh, yes, I
know why. I know . . . but when you are mad
you can't stop to reason. We look at it this
way. . . . When we're not mad, from having
been too many days under fire . . . we say, as
we talk it over. . . . There are the English . . .
they've done splendidly . . . they've taken two
years, it is true, to get their army really in shape
. . . but they didn't have anything to begin with
. . . they're fine . . . all that we could expect.
But all the same, during the two years, Frenchmen were dying like flies . . . just watering the
whole North with blood . . . yes, I've seen a
brook run red just like the silly poems that no-
body believed. And the Americans . . . yes
. . . suppose this man and I should get to quar-
relling. Of course you can't jump right in and
decide which is to blame, if you don't know much
about the beginning. You *have* to stand off and
watch, and see which fights fair, and all the rest
. . . *but while you are deciding, all France is
dying.* It is time the weight of the defence is
taken off France . . . there won't be any French-

men left alive in France . . . and here she is
with all these foreigners over-running her! Do
you suppose they are going to leave after the
war? Not much. All these Algerians and
Senegals and Anamites — not to speak of the
Belgians and English and Americans . . . there
won't be any Frenchmen left alive, and France
will be populated by foreigners . . . *that's* what
we have to look forward to for all the reward of
our blood. They keep promising help, but they
don't bring it. *We* have to go back and go back!
I tell you, Ma'ame, *three years is too long a time!*
No man can stand three years of war! It makes
you into somebody else . . . you've died so many
times you're like a walking corpse . . . isn't that
just how you feel?' he appealed to his companion, who said impassively,

"'No, damn you, that isn't a bit how I feel.
I just say to myself, *" It's war,"* and *" That's
the way war is,"* and I don't *try* to make anything
out of it the way you do. That's silly! You
just have to stick it out. Understanding it hasn't
anything to do with it.'

" The first one went off on another tack . . .
still wilder and more incoherent. ' It's the capitalists . . . that's what it is . . . they saw that
the people . . . the proletariat . . . that's *me,*'

with a thump of his fist on his chest, ' had begun to see too clearly how things were going and so they stirred up this hornet's nest to blind everybody . . . for in war even more than in peace (and that's saying a good deal) . . . it's the proletariat that bears the burdens.   Who do you think is in the trenches now . . . is the bourgeois class? *No!* It's the labouring class.   One by one, the bourgeois have slipped out of it.   Got themselves the fat jobs at the rear, work in hospitals . . . anything but to stay out in the front-line trenches with us poor rats of working-people! Isn't that so?'

" He appealed to his companion, who answered again very calmly (it was extraordinary how they didn't seem to mind differing diametrically from each other.   I suppose they had the long habit of arguing together).   ' No, it's not so!   In my company there are as many bourgeois as labouring men.'

" The first man never paid the least attention to these brief denials of everything he was saying. ' It's the proletariat that always pays . . . isn't it so, Ma'ame!   Peace or war, old times or new, it's always the poor who pay all the debts!   And they're doing it to such a tune now in France that there won't be any left, when the war is over . . .

oh, it's got to stop. There's no use talking about it . . . and it *will,* too, one of these days . . . who *cares* how it stops! Life . . . any sort of life . . . is better than anything else.'

" At this the other soldier said, ' Don't pay any attention to him, Madame, he always goes on so . . . but he'll stick it out just the same. We all will. That's the nature of the Frenchman, Madame. He must have his grievance. He must grumble and grumble but when it's necessary, he goes forward just the same. . . . Only he has to talk such a lot before! '

" ' Oh, yes, we'll *hold* them, fast enough! ' agreed the first one. ' We'll never let them get past us! ' (This type of declaring poilu is much given to contradicting himself flatly!) ' But never, never, *never* an offensive again, from the French . . . you *see,* Madame — Never again an offensive from the French! They've done their share! They've done more than their share. Never an offensive. We'll hold till the Americans get here, but not more! '

" We were pulling into the station at Meaux by this time, and as the train stood there waiting, I heard a sound that brought my heart up into my mouth . . . the sound of a lot of young men's voices singing an American College song!

Everybody sprang to the windows and there was a group of American boys, in their nice new uniforms, singing at the tops of their voices, and putting their heads together like a college glee-club. Their clear young voices completely filled that great smoky station and rang out with the most indescribably confident inspiriting effect! 'Good God!' cried the dingy, battered soldier at my elbow, 'how little they know what they are going into!' The soldier from Bourgogne said nothing, but looked very stern and sad. The contrast between those two men, one so rebellious, the other so grimly enduring, both so shabby and war-worn, and those splendidly fresh boys outside, seemed to me the most utterly symbolic episode imaginable. There was America — there was France.

"It changed the current of the talk. After that we talked all together, the two bourgeois joining in . . . sober talk enough, of probabilities and hopes and fears.

"As I walked home at one o'clock in the morning through the silent black streets of Paris, turning over and over what that poor disinherited slum-dweller had said as we parted, quite earnestly and simply as he had poured out all his disgust and revolt, 'Good-bye, Ma'ame, I never

met an American before. I hope I'll meet many
more. You tell the Americans the *French will
see it through* . . . if a new offensive is necessary . . . we'll do it! It's the only chance any-
body has to have a world fit to live in!'"

When she had finished her story, Dorothy
Canfield concluded something like this: "That's
what they all come back to, after their fit of utter
horror at their life is over. It does them good,
apparently, to talk it all out to a patient listener.
They always, always end by saying that even what
they are living through is better than a world com-
manded by the Germans . . . what a perfectly
amazing distrust that nation has accumulated
against itself!"

They are sick of war; war weary and sad.
Yet they will fight on. The will to fight is outside the individual will; yet it is not the will of
the leaders, nor is it the will of the many com-
bined in a common will. For the many are tired
unto death of war. But for all that they will
fight on without flinching. It is the national will
— the will deeper than the will of leaders,
stronger than the molten will of the many in one
purpose. It is the tradition of centuries; it is the
unexpressed purpose, perhaps unconscious habit
of an old, old people, united far down in the

roots of them; not so much by race, for the Franks are of many breeds; not so much by industrial or geographical ties or even political unity, though it approaches that; but bound most surely by the sense of national tradition. A people is fighting. From a thousand villages with their primeval temples, with their lovely cathedrals grown out of the hearts of the race buried in the shadow of their spires, from the shining rivers that flow through green pastures, from soft hills rich in folk tales of heroes, come the millions; and from Paris, ever radiant in her venerable youth, come other millions who make this fighting soul of the nation. What if it grumbles as it fights; it will still fight on. Of course it is sick of war; but it will not stop. It is a spirit that is fighting in France, the spirit of a brave people.

We have in France a few hundred thousand men and will soon have a million and more who are offering their lives in Service. But the whole French nation is giving thus. And it is without hate. One finds instead of hatred in France a feeling of deep disgust for the German and all his works. The spirit of the French is not vicious. It is beautiful. When the war ceases that may subside, may retire to the under con-

sciousness of the people. But it will not depart.
It also will remain eternally a part of the salvage
of this war.

By the time the transgression of our car had
been sufficiently atoned for, dusk was falling.
And Henry broke away from the gothic arches
of the trees and made for a tavern. He had
learned that one must take food in France where
he can find it, and ten minutes later we came upon
him in front of the inn, talking in a slow loud
voice to what was either the inn-keeper's daughter
or his pretty young wife thus: " I said," Henry
paused and nodded his head and beat the thing
in with his hand; " we want some supper — de
jurnay — toot sweet! " She shook her head and
shrugged her shoulders very prettily and said she
could not " say pa." And Henry laughed and
went on, still enunciating each word distinctly.
" Ah, don't tell us you can't ' Say pa ': say ' wee
wee.' " And again he told her " toot sweet."
That was the only part of the French language
that Henry was entirely sure of — that and
" comb be-ah! " But we could not get it through
her head. So we loaded ourselves into the car
and headed back for St. Dizier, where at least
they understood Henry's gestures, and we could
get food!

Our next journey took us to the greatest training camp in the allied part of the world. It is not the largest camp, of course. It accommodates less than twenty thousand soldiers. But it is what might be called the post graduate college of all training camps. Here ten thousand men come every week from other training camps all over the earth, and are given intensive training. For six days, eighteen and twenty hours a day, these soldiers, trained by many months' labour on other fields, are given the Ph.D. in battle lore, and are turned out the seventh day after a Saturday night lecture on hate, and shot straight up to the front. In all France there is no more grisly place for the weak-stomached man than this training camp — not even the front line trenches will kick up his gorge more sedulously. Yet at first sight the place looks innocent enough. One sees a great basin hollowed among the hills, and in the ten thousand acre plain one sees horsemen galloping, soldiers running, great trucks and tanks lumbering over the field; men digging, men throwing hand-grenades, men clambering over trench walls, stumbling over crater holes, men doing all the innumerable things that are learned by those who carry on the handicraft of war.

But when one starts with the first class and

goes along through the day's work with it, the deadly seriousness of the training gets to him. The first thing the first class does is to gather around a sergeant major, who in a few simple words tells his pupils how to use the bayonet. Then they go out and use the bayonet as he has taught them. Then the pupils gather around another sergeant major, who tells them how to use the hand-grenade or the knife or the butt of a gun, and the simple-hearted lads go out and use the grenade, the knife, or the butt of the gun. At length they are taken to a part of the ground where some trenches are sunken in the earth. Before the trenches are barbed wire entanglements and deep jagged shell craters. The imitation enemy trenches badly bombed by barrage lie twenty rods beyond. The men are taken in hand by the amiable sergeant major and taught to yell and roar, and growl and snarl, to simulate the most murderous passion, and the simulation of a husky youth in his twenties of a murderous passion is realistic enough to make your flesh creep; for the very simulation produces the passion, as every wise man's son doth know. Then the youths are lined up in the trench, and numbered " one-two; one-two; one-two "; clear down the trench. Then the order is given to go over the top. Every gun rattles on the trench-top, and the second lieutenant goes over. In the English papers the list of dead begins " Second lieutenant, unless otherwise designated." And in the war zone the second lieutenants are known as " The suicides' club." Well, the second lieutenants get on top, and, down in the trench, number one hands his leg to number two; clear down the line; number two boosts number one to the top, then number one lends a hand to number two and pulls him out. Meanwhile enemy fire is hot. The line forms in open order. The blood curdling yells begin — and mingle in an animal roar that sounds like the howl of an orang-outang in the circus just before it is fed at the after-show! It is the voice of hell. Then the line walks — not runs, but walks under machine gun and shell fire to the enemy trench; for experience has proven that if the men run into that fire they will be out of breath and probably go down in the hand-to-hand, knee-to-knee, eye-to-eye conflict with knife and bayonet and gun butt that always occurs when they go over the top to charge the enemy trench. As they near the enemy trench the bestial howl rises, and as they jump into the shell-shattered trenches the howl is maniacal. In the trenches are canvas bags made to represent wounded enemies. The first wave over the top leaves these bags for the stretcher bearers. But by the time the next wave comes over, or the third wave comes, the stretcher bearers are supposed to have cleared the trenches of wounded enemies, and after that every soldier is supposed to jab his bayonet in every bag in the trenches, as he is expected to jab every dead body, to prevent an enemy from playing possum and then getting to a presumably disabled enemy machine gun and shooting our soldiers in the back. Every time a student soldier jabs a canvas bag he snarls and growls like a jackal, and if he misses a bag it counts against him in the day's markings. Wave after wave comes over, and prisoners are sent to the rear, if there are guards to take them. If not prisoners are killed, and one does not waste ammunition on them. It may be well to pause here to say that in the gentle art of murdering the business of taking prisoners is not elaborately worked out. They learn that by rote, rather than by note. The Canadians, since two of their men were crucified by the Prussians, take few Prussian prisoners. Here is a snap-back of the film. It is the Rue di Rivoli in Paris. Two lanky youngsters in Canadian uniform are talking to Henry and me.

"What part of the states do you Canadians come from?" we ask. They grin and answer, "San Francisco."

WE: "What's this story about you Canadians not taking any prisoners?"

THEY: "Oh, we take prisoners — all right, I guess!"

WE: "Well, how often?"

THEY: "Oh, sometimes."

WE: "Come on now, boys, as Californians to Kansans, tell us the truth."

The tall one looked at the short one for permission to tell the truth, and got it. Then he said:

"Well, it's like this. We go into a trench after them damn brutes has been playing machine guns on us, knowing as soon as we get in they'll surrender, but trying to kill as many of us as they can before they give up. Then they raise up their hands and begin yelling, 'Kamerade, Kamerade,' and someone says, 'Come on, fellers, let's take this poor beggar,' and we're about to do it when along comes a chap and sees this devil, and up goes a gun by the barrel, and whack it comes down on the Boche's head, and the feller says, 'No, damn him, he killed my pal,' and we

" What part of the States do you Canadians come
from? "

polishes him off! polishes him off and cleans out the trench."

WE: "Now, boys, does that always happen? How often do you fellows polish Fritzie off and clean up the trench?"

THEY (after the short one had nodded to the tall one): "Well, mister, I'll tell you. It's got so it's mighty damn risky for any Prussian to surrender to any Canadian!"

When the line out there in the training camp has gone to its objective, which usually is the third or fourth enemy trench, the men begin digging in. Then they go back to the sergeant major for more instructions. The digging in is usually done under a curtain of fire to protect them. It is a great picture.

In another part of the field we saw the engineers learning to make tunnels under the enemy; saw the engineers blowing up enemy trenches — a pleasant and exciting spectacle; saw the engineers making camouflage, and it may interest the gentle reader to know that one of the niftiest bits of camouflage we saw was over a French seventy-five gun. It was set in the field. A railroad siding ran to it. On a canvas over the gun two rails and the usual number of ties were painted, and the track ran on beyond. Fifty feet in the air one could not tell that the gun was there.

The liveliest part of this martial cloister was the section devoted to the bayonet practice. And as we watched the men trying to rip the vest buttons off a dummy and expose its gastric arrangements with a bayonet, while loping along at full speed, we recalled a Civil War story which may well be revived here. A Down-easter from Vermont and a Southerner were going around and around one day at Shiloh, each trying to get the other with the bayonet, but both were good dodgers. Finally as the Yankee was getting winded he cried between puffs:

" Watch aout —! Mind what yer dewin'! Ye dern smart aleck! Haint yew got no sense! You'll stick the pint of thet thing in my boawels, if you ain't keerful! "

We heard a lot of shivery stories around that training camp. They told us that the French chasseurs, the famous blue devils, were more or less careless about the way they forgot to take prisoners. They are a proud people, from the French Alps, and exceedingly democratic. A German brigadier, caught under their barrage, came up to a troop of chasseurs and when they demanded his surrender asked curtly, " Where's your superior officer? " They pointed down the hill, and he started down. At a safe distance they threw a hand grenade into him and obliterated him, remarking, " Well, the world is that much safer for democracy." It is told of a Canadian who came across a squad of Germans with their hands up that he asked: " How many are you? " Eleven, they said. He reached in his pocket; found his hand grenade, and threw it at them, remarking, "I'm sorry I have but the one; but divide it between you!" There is also the story of the Indian Sikhs, who begged to go out on a night raiding party — crawling on their bellies with their knives as their only weapons. Finally two of them returned with new pairs of boots. Showing them proudly to their amazed Captain, they said humbly, " Yes, sire! But you would be pained to learn how long we had to hunt for a fit!" There is also the story of the festive Tommy who tried to play a practical joke on his German prisoner by slipping a lighted bomb in the German's pocket. The Tommy then started to run; the German thought he must keep up with his captor and Tommy realized that the joke was on him, just as the bomb went off and killed them both.

Such stories are innumerable.   They are probably untrue.   But they indicate what men at war
think is funny; they reflect a certain impoliteness
and lack of courtesy that prevails in war.   As it
wears on it grows more or less unneighbourly.
And yet the upheaval of war is just a passing
emotional disturbance in the normal life of men.
Even in France, even in the war zone, there is no
glorifying of war; men in war, at least on our side
of the line, hate war more than they hate the Germans.   And with the whole heart of the civilized
world — if one frankly may call the Turk and the
Prussian the savages that they are — set upon
maintaining this war to a victory for the allies,
civilization may be said to be in the war as a make-
shift.   Everywhere one hears that it is a war
against war.   Every one is " longing for the dawn
of peace " when it shall come with justice, and in
the meantime France is as deeply devoted to healing the wounds of war as it is in promoting the
war.   Six hundred French societies are devoted to
various war works of mercy!   Every man and
woman in France who is not a soldier or a nurse
is working in one of these societies.   And yet
life goes on with all this maladjustment of its
cams and cogs and levers much as in its ordinary routine.   There never were more joyous

dahlias and phlox and china asters than we saw coming back from that training camp where men were learning the big death game. And when we came to Paris the real business of war seemed remote. Of course, Paris is affected by the war. But Paris is not war-like. One doesn't associate Paris with " grim-visaged war ! " For if Paris is not gay, still it remains mighty amiable. At noon the boulevard cafés are filled to the side-walks, and until nine o'clock at night they give a fair imitation of their former happiness. Then they close and the picture shows are crowded, and the theaters are filled. One sees soldiers and their women folk at the opera and at the vaudeville shows more than at the other shows. During the summer and the autumn a strong man put on a show at the Follies with the soldiers that was the talk of the town. His game was a tug of war. He announced that he would give fifty dol-lars to any soldier who could withstand him. The strong man sat the soldier down on the floor, foot to foot before him. Both grasped a pole, and it was the strong man's " act " to throw the soldier over his head, on to a mattress just back of the strong man. It is a simple act; one that soon would tire Broadway, but when one remem-bers that soldiers bring their local pride with them

to Paris from the ends of the earth, from New
Zealand, from India, from Canada, from South
Africa, from Morocco, from China, from Aus-
tralia, and then when one remembers that the
men of his country are gathered in the theater
to back every local athlete, it is easy to see why
the strong man holds week after week, month
after month, season after season.   Every night
some proud nation gathers in the show house to
get that fifty dollars with its favourite son.   And
every night some favourite son almost gets it.
And if the strong man didn't fudge a little, pinch
the favourite son's hands on the pole and make
him let go, almost every night the strong man
would be worsted.   The struggle sets the house
yelling.   It is the only real drama in Paris.   We
noticed that the shows of Paris which appealed
to the eyes and ears were far below the American
standard.   In comedy which appeals to something behind the sense, in the higher grades of
acting, the Paris shows were, on the whole, better
than Broadway shows.   But in the choruses, the
dancers lack that finish, that top dressing of me-
chanical unison required by American taste.
Moreover the lighting and colour were poor.
The music at the Follies was Victor Herbert
of 1911! Old American popular songs seemed

to be in vogue. One heard " O Johnny " and " Over There " at every vaudeville house this year. Sometimes they were done in French, sometimes in English. In Genoa, one may say in passing that we heard one of the songs from " Hitchy-Coo " done in Italian. It was eery! American artists are popular in Paris. We saw a girl at three show houses in Paris, under the name of Betty Washington, doing a gipsy dance, playing the fiddle. She was barefoot, and Henry, who has a keen eye, noticed that she had her toes rouged! But she always was good for four encores, and she usually got a good start at the fifth from Henry and me; we had just that much national pride! Great throngs of soldiers filled these gay show houses. The French, the English, and the Australians seemed satisfied with them. But the Canadians and Americans sniffed. To them Paris is a poor show town.

One night we fell into a Boulevard show the like of which we had never seen before. It was a political revue! The whole evening was devoted to skits directed at the ministry, at the food administration, at the scandals in the interior department and the deputies, at the high taxes and the profiteering of the munition makers. The skits were done in dialogue, song and dance, and the various forms of burlesque. A good crowd — but not a soldier crowd — sat through it and applauded appreciatively. Imagine an American audience devoting a whole evening to a theatrical performance exclusively concerned with Hoover, Secretary Daniels, Colonel Roosevelt, former Mayor Mitchel, and LaFollette. In America we get little politics out of the theater. In France, where they distrust the newspapers, they get much politics from the theater. The theater is free in France — and apparently not so closely censored as the newspapers. We learned that night at the revue of a coming cabinet crisis, before the newspapers announced it. And in learning of the crisis we had this curious social experience, which we modestly hoped was quite as Parisian as the Revue. During the first act of the show it was Greek to Henry and me. We could understand a vaudeville show, and by following the synopsis could poke along after the pantomime in a comedy. But here in this revue, where the refinements of sarcasm and satire were at play and that without a cue, we were stumped. Henry was for getting out and going somewhere else. But we had a dollar a seat in the show and it seemed to me that patience would bring results. And it did! A good-looking, middle-aged couple sat down in the seats next to us, and the woman began talking English. She was sitting next to me, so it was my turn, not Henry's to speak. We asked her if it would be too much trouble to interpret the show for two jays from Middle Western America. She replied cordially enough. And she gave us a splendid running interpretation of the show. The man with her seemed friendly. We noticed that he was slyly holding her hand in the dark, and that once he slipped his arm around her when the lights went clear down. But that spelled a newly married middle-aged couple, and we would have bet money that he was a widower and she, late from his office, was at the head of his household. Between acts he and Henry went out to smoke, leaving me with the lady. We exchanged confidences of one sort and another after the manner of strangers in a strange land. When it occurred to me to ask: " What does your husband do for a living? "

" My — what? " she exclaimed.

" Your husband, there? "

" Who — that man? Why, I never saw him in my life until I picked him up in a café an hour ago! "

And she got from me a somewhat gaspy " Oh." But we had a good chat just the same and she told me all about the coming fall of the cabinet. Her type in America would not be interested in politics. But the shows of the boulevards discuss politics and the theaters are free! So her type in France had to know politics. It takes all kinds of people and also all kinds of peoples to make a world. And the war really is being fought so that they may work out their lives and their national traditions freely and after the call of their own blood. If we are to have only one kind of people, the kind is easy to find. There is kultur!

Still the love affairs of the French did bother us. Henry did not mind them so much; but to me they seemed as unreasonable and as improbable as the ocean and onion soup seemed to Henry. Every man has his aversion, and the French idea of separating love from marriage, and establishing it beautifully in another relation, is my aversion, and it will have to stand. Henry was patient with me, but we were both genuinely glad when a day or two later we came back to the sprightly little American love affair that we had chaperoned on the *Espagne* crossing the ocean. That love affair we could understand. It had been following us with a feline tenacity all over France. When we left the Eager Soul with the

Gilded Youth in the hospital at — we'll say Landrecourt, because that is not the place — we thought our love affair was gone for ever. The letter she gave us to deliver to the Young Doctor we had to trust to other hands; for he was not at the American hospital where he should have been. He had gone to the British front for a week's experimental work in something with four syllables and a Latin name at that. But the cat came back one day, when we were visiting a hospital four hours out of Paris. The place had that curious French quality of charm about it, which we Americans do not manage to put into our " places and palaces." Down a winding village street — a kind of low-walled stone canyon, narrow and grey, but brightened with uniforms like the streets of most French villages these days — we wormed our machine and stopped at an important looking building — an official looking building. It was not official, we learned — just a château. A driveway ran under it. That got us. For when a road leads into a house in America, it means a jail, or a courthouse, or a hotel, or a steel magnate's home or a department store. But when we scooted under the house we came into a wide white courtyard, gravel paved. We left the machine and went from the court-

yard into a garden — the loveliest old walled garden imaginable.   At the corners of the garden
were fine old trees — tall, spike-shaped ever-
greens of some variety, and in the midst of it was
a weeping yew tree and a fountain.   Around the
walls were shrubs and splashed about the walks
and near the fountain were gorgeous dabs of
colour, phlox and asters, and dahlias and holly-
hocks and flowers of various gay sorts.   And
back of the garden, down a shaded path, lay the
hospital — a new modern barracks of a hospital,
in a field sheltered from the street by all that
grandeur and all that beauty.   The hospital was
made of rough, brown stained boards; it was one
story high, built architecturally like a tannery,
and camouflaged as to the roof to represent
" green fields and running brooks."   Board floors
and board partitions under the roof were covered
as well as they could be; and stoves furnished the
heat.   The beds — acres and acres of iron beds
— were assembled in the great wards and
stretched far down the long rooms like white
ranks of skeletoned ghosts.   The place was
American — new, excruciatingly clean, and was
run like a factory.   We were proud of it, and
of the business-like young medical students who
as orderlies and bookkeepers and helpers went

about in their brand new uniforms — young
crown princes of democracy, twice as handsome
and three times as dignified as they would have
been if they had royal blood.   Henry called them
the heirs apparent " of all the ages " and enjoyed
them greatly.   They certainly gave the place a
tone, converting a sprawling ugly pile of brown
boards into a king's palace.   When we had finished our errand at the hospital and were returning through the garden, we met our young doctor.
He was sitting on an old stone bench, among
the asters and dahlias — wounded.   It was not a
serious wound from an ordinary man's stand-
point; but from the Young Doctor's it was grave
indeed.   For it was a bullet wound through his
hand.   He thought it would not affect the mus-
cles permanently — but no one could know.
Then he sat there in the mediaeval garden among
the flowers under the yew trees and told us how
it happened; took us out to the first aid post
again, and on out to the first line trenches, and
over them into No Man's Land, stumbling over
the dead, helping the stretcher bearers with the
wounded.   In time he came to a wounded German — a Prussian officer with a shell-wound in
his leg.

He told us what happened, impersonally, as

one who is listening to another man's story in his own mouth. "I gave him something like a first aid to stop the bleeding," the young Doctor paused, picked a ravelling from his bandage and went on, still detached from the narrative. "Then I put my arm around him, to help him back to the ambulance." Again he hesitated and said quietly, "That was a half mile back and the shells were still popping — more or less — around us." He looked for appreciation of the situation. He got it, smiled and went on without lifting his voice. "Then he did it."

"Not that fellow?" exclaimed Henry.

"Well, how?" from me.

"Oh, I don't know. He just did it," droned the Young Doctor. "We were talking along; and then he seemed to quit talking. I looked up. The pistol was at my head; I knocked it away as he fired. It got my hand!" He stopped, began poking the gravel with his toe, and smiled again as one who has heard an old story and wants to be polite. To Henry and me, it was unbelievable. We sat down on the hoary, moss-covered curb of the ancient fountain regardless of our spanking new uniforms and cried: "Well, my Heavenly home!" He nodded, drew a deep breath and said, "That's the how of it."

He told us what happened impersonally as one who is
listening to another man's story in his own mouth

" Well, what do you know about —"

Then Henry checked me with, " You weren't expecting it? Did he make no warning sign? "

" Not a peep — not a chirrup," answered the Doctor, still diffidently. Then he added, as one reflecting over an incident in a rather remote past: " It was odd, wasn't it. You would think that two men who stood where we were together — I, who had put my hands in his live flesh, and had felt his blood flow through my fingers, and he who was clinging to my body for support — you would think we had come together not as foes, but as friends; for the war was over for him! "

The Young Doctor's eyebrows knitted. His mouth set. He went on: " This man should have abandoned his military conscience. But no —," the Doctor shook his head sadly, " he was a Prussian before he was a man! He carefully figured it out, that it takes four years to make a doctor, and three months to make a soldier, so to kill a doctor is as good as killing a dozen men. It's all very scientific, this German warfare — scientific and fanatical; Nietzsche and Mahomet, what a perfect alliance it is between the Kaiser and the Sultan."

Then it came to us again that Germans, on seas,

in submarines, in air, in their planes bombing hospitals, and on land, looting and dynamiting villages — in all their martial enterprises, think unlike the rest of civilized men. They are a breed apart — savage, material-minded, diabolic, unrestrained by fear or love of God, man or devil. We talked of these things for a time; but something, the quiet beauty of the garden maybe, took the edge off our hate. And gradually it became apparent to me, at least, that the Young Doctor was marking time until we should have the sense to tell him something of the Eager Soul. What did he care for the war? For the Prussians? For their Babylonian philosophy? For his wounded hand? What were gardens made for in this drab earth, if not for sanctuaries of lovers? One does not go to a garden to hate, to buy, or sell, to fight, to philosophize, but to adore something or someone, somehow or somewhere. And the Young Doctor was in his Holy Temple, and we knew it. So Henry asked: "You received your letter?" And when he thanked us for our trouble, Henry asked again: "Did she tell you that the Gilded Youth was there at her hospital?"

"Only in a pencilled postscript after she had

decided to send the letter to me by you," answered the Doctor.

That sounded good to me. Evidently she had written to the Young Doctor before the Gilded Youth had appeared. Also presumably she had not written to the Gilded Youth. If she had written to him after the air raid that had killed the head nurse, it would indicate that she had turned to the Young Doctor, in an emotional crisis, and that he was still a safe bet, as against the Gilded Youth. The only question which occurred to me to develop this fact was this: " Did she tell you that she was made assistant to the new head nurse that came to supply the place of the one who was slain by the Germans?" Henry looked at me as if he thought the question was unfair.

" Yes," laughed the Doctor, " in the very first line."

" What odds are you giving now, Bill?" asked Henry bitterly.

" In the very first line,—" we could all three see the Eager face, the proud blue eyes, the pretty effective hands brushing the straying crinkly strands of red hair from her forehead, as she sat there in the bare little nurses' room, bringing her first promotion in pride to the young Doctor. Perhaps he did not realize all that it meant. For you see he was very young. Certainly he did not understand about the odds and repeated the word in a question. Henry cut in, " Oh, nothing, only that night after they went walking in the hospital yard, Bill made me give him three to five. Now I ought to have two to one. It's all over but the shouting." And Henry laughed at the Young Doctor's bewilderment; but the young Doctor looked at his bandaged hand and shook his head. The walk in the hospital yard was disturbing news to him.

" Ah, don't worry about that," Henry reassured him. " Why, man, you ought to have heard what she said about you ! " And Henry, being a good-natured sort, told the Doctor what the Eager Soul had said to the Gilded Youth in the hospital compound, while the buzzing monsters in the air were singing their nightingale songs of death in the moonlight.

We left the Young Doctor after he had squeezed out of us all the news we had of the girl. Long after we had passed through the garden gate, out into the white, gravel-paved court under the proud arch and into the crooked, low, grey-walled canyon of the street, we thought of the Young Doctor sitting there reading blue eyes into china asters, red hair into dahlias, pink cheeks into the phlox, and hearing ineffable things whispered among the leaves of the melancholy yew tree. And all that, in a land of waste and desolation, with war's alarms on every wind.

And we thought that he looked more like a poet than a Doctor even in his uniform; and less like a soldier than either. Such is the alchemy of love in youth!

CHAPTER VI

WHEREIN WE BECOME A TRIO AND JOURNEY
TO ITALY

A S the autumn deepened we found our Red
Cross work ending. This work had taken
Henry and me from our quiet country newspaper offices in Kansas and had suddenly plunged
us into the turmoil of the big war. For days and
days we had been riding in motor cars along the
line in France from Rouen to Bacarat and often
ambulances had hauled us — always more or less
frightened — up near the trenches of the front
line. We had tramped through miles of hospitals and had snuggled eagerly into the little
dugouts and caves that made the first aid posts.
We had learned many new and curious things —
most of which were rather useless in publishing
the Wichita *Beacon* or the Emporia *Gazette;* as,
for instance, how to wear a gas mask, how to fire
a trench mortar, how to look through a trench
periscope, and how to duck when a shell comes

in. Also we had stood god-father to a serial love affair that began on the boat coming over and was for ever being " continued in our next." And it was all — riding along the line, huddling in abris, sneaking scared to death along trenches, and ducking from the shells — all vastly diverting. We had grown fat on it; not that we needed just that expression of felicity, having four hundred pounds between us. But it was almost finished and we were sadly turning our faces westward to our normal and reasonably honest lives at home, when Medill McCormick came to Paris and tempted us to go to Italy. It was a great temptation; " beyond the Alps lies Italy," as a copy book sentence has lure in it, and as a possible journey to a new phase of the war, it caught us; and we started.

So we three stood on the platform, at the station at Modane, in Savoy, a few hundred yards from the Italian border, one fair autumn day, and our heavy clothes — two Red Cross uniforms and a pea-green hunting suit, made us sweat copiously and unbecomingly. The two Red Cross uniforms belong to Henry and me; the pea-green hunting outfit belonged to Medill McCormick, congressman at large from Illinois, U. S. A. He was going into Italy to study the situation. As

a congressman he felt that he should be really
informed about the war as it was the most vital
subject upon which he should have to vote. So
there we stood, two Kansas editors, and an Illinois congressman, while the uniforms of the continent brushed by us, in uniforms ourselves, after
a fashion, but looking conspicuously civilian, and
incorrigibly middle western. Medill in his pea-
green hunting outfit looked more soldierly than
we. For although we wore Sam Browne belts,
to indicate that we were commissioned officers —
commissioned as Red Cross Colonels — and although we wore Parisian uniforms of correct
cut, we knew in our hearts that they humped in
the back and flopped in the front, and sagged at
the shoulders. A fat man can't wear the modern American army uniform without looking like
a sack of meal. Henry fell to calling the tunics
our Mother Hubbards. We looked long and en-
viously at the slim-waisted boys in khaki; but we
never could get their god-like effects. For alas,
the American uniform is high-waisted, and a fat
man never was designed for a Kate Greenaway!
So we paced the platform at Modane trying to
look unconcerned while the soldiers of France,
Italy, Russia, Belgium, England and Rumania
walked by us, clearly wondering what form of

A fat man can't wear the modern American Army
uniform without looking like a sack of meal

military freak we were. For the American Red Cross uniform was not so familiar in those latitudes as it was to be a month later, when Major Murphy came swinging through Modane with forty-eight carloads of Red Cross supplies, a young army of Red Cross nurses and workers, and half a million dollars in ready cash to spend upon the stricken cities of Northern Italy choked with refugees fleeing before the German invasion! Today, the American flag floats from a hundred flag-poles in Italian cities, from Venice to Naples. Under that flag the American Red Cross has soup kitchens, food stations, aid bureaus for civilian relief all along the line of the invader in Italy, and the Red Cross uniform which made the soldiers' eyes bug out there at the border in the early autumn, now is familiar and welcome in Italy. But we three unsoldierly looking civilians took that uniform into a strange country.

Our first evening in Italy was spent in Genoa. And coming direct from Paris, where men out of uniform were few, the thing that opened our mouths in wonder was the number of men we saw. There were worlds and worlds of men in Genoa; men in civilian clothes. The streets were black with men. Straw hats, two piece suits, gay neckties — things which were as remote from France

as from Mars, figures that recalled the ancient
days of one's youth, before the war; days in New
York, for instance, where men in straw hats and
white crash were common.   These things we saw
with amazement in Genoa!   And then our eyes
caught the flashy bands on their arms — bands
that indicated that these men are in the industrial
reserves, not drafted because they are doing industrial war work.   But for all of these industrial reservists there was an overplus of men in
Genoa.   It is a seaport and there were " the market girls and fishermen, the shepherds and the
sailors, too," a crowd gathered from the world's
ends, and we sat under the deep arches before a
gay café, listened to New York musical hits from
the summer's roof gardens, and watched the
show.   In that day — only three weeks before
the German invasion — the war was a long way
from Genoa.   At the next table to us an American sea-faring man was telling an English naval
officer about the adventures of three sailing ships
which had bested two submarines three days before in the Mediterranean; some Moroccan sailors
were flirting across two tables with some pretty
Piedmontese girls, and inside the café, the harp,
the flute and the violin were doing what they
could to make all our hearts beat young!   A pic-

ture show across the street sprayed its gay crowd
over the sidewalks and a vaudeville house down
stairs gathered up rivulets of humanity from the
spray.   Somewhere near by was a dance, for we
heard the rhythmic swish and lisp of young feet
and the gay cry of the music.   Here and there
came a soldier; sometimes we saw a woman in
mourning; but uniforms and mourners were un-
common.   The war was a tale that is told.

But the next day in Rome the war moved into
our vision again.   But even if Rome was more
visibly martial than Genoa, still it was not Paris.
One could see gay colours upon women in Rome;
one might see straw hats upon the men, and in
the stores and shops the war did not fill every
·window as it filled the shop windows of Paris.
Rome was taking the war seriously, of course, but
the war was not the tragedy to Rome before the
invasion that it was to France.

Yet there was to me a change in Rome — from
the Rome one knew who had been there eight
years before — a change stranger and deeper than
the change one felt in coming from Rome to
Paris.   This new Rome was a cleaner Rome, a
more prosperous Rome, a happier Rome.   Something had been happening to the people.   They
wore better clothes, they seemed to live in cleaner

tenements; they certainly had a different squint at life from the Romans of the first decade of this century. One heard two answers to the question that arose in one's heart. One group said: " It is prosperity. Italy never has seen such prosperity as she has seen during the past ten years. There has been work for everyone, and work at good wages. So you see the working people well-clad, well-housed, clean and contented." Another answered the question thus: " The Socialists have done it. We have had plenty of work in other years; but we have worked for small wages, and have lived in squalor. We still work as we always have worked, but we get better pay, and we get our better pay in many ways; first in relatively higher wages, next in safeguards thrown around labour, and restrictions on the predatory activities of capital. The Socialists in government have forced many reforms in housing, in labour conditions, in the distribution of the profits of labour and capital, and we are living in hope of better things rather than in fear of worse!" One may take his choice of answers; probably the truth lies between the two. Prosperity has done something; socialism in government has done something, and each has promoted the other!

But the war has done one thing to Rome indisputably. It has paralysed the tourist business. Rome was the greatest tourist city in the world. But now her boarding houses and her ruins are deserted. Occasionally in the shops one sees that mother and daughter, wistful, eager, half-starved for every good thing in life, expatriated, living shabbily in the upper regions of some respectable pension, detached from the world about them, uprooted from the world at home, travel-jaded, ruin-sated, picture-wise and unbelievably stupid concerning life's real interests — the mother and daughter who in the old days lived so numerously amid the splendours of Europe, flitting from Rome to Florence, from Florence to Lucerne, from Lucerne to Berlin, and thence to Paris and London, following the seasons like the birds. But today war prices have sent that precious pair home, and let us hope to honest work. It is a comfort to see Rome without their bloodless faces! That much the war has done for democracy at any rate!

And the passing of this " relic of old dacincy," the shabby genteel of the earth from Rome — even if the passing is a temporary social phenomenon, has a curious symbolic timeliness, coming when the working class is rising. It leaves

Rome almost as middle class as Kansas City and Los Angeles! For in Rome one feels that the upper class, the ruling class of other centuries, is weaker than it is elsewhere in the world. They tell you flippantly that the king is training his son to run for president. The high caste Romans have an Austrian pride, that " goeth before destruction." For politically their power is sadly on the wane. They are miserably moth-eaten compared to our own arrogant princes of Wall Street or even compared to the dazed dukes and earls of England, who are looking out at the wreck of matter and the crash of worlds about them. One feels vaguely that these Italian nobles are passing through a rather mean stage of decay. For a time during the latter part of the last century and during the first decade of this century, the Italian noblemen tried to edge into business. They lent their names to promotion schemes, and the schemes, upon the whole, turned out badly, and the people learned to distrust all financial schemes under noble patronage; so the nobility is going to work. A few strong families remain — the present royal house of Savoy is among the strong ones.

Our business led us to a call on the Duke of Genoa, uncle to the King, who in the King's absence at the front with his soldiers, was a sort of acting king on the job in Rome. The automobile took us into the first court of the Royal Palace. Now the Royal Palace — save for a few executive offices — has been turned into an army hospital and we saw doctors and nurses dodging in and out of the innumerable corridors, and smelled iodoform everywhere. A major domo, in scarlet, who seemed in the modern disinfected smell of the place like the last guard of mediaevalism, greeted us as we alighted from our car; a great, powerful soldier he was, with white and gold on his scarlet broadcloth. He showed us into a passage where the minister waited who was to take us to the Duke. The minister led us down a long stately gallery, out of the twentieth century into the fifteenth, where at the end of the gallery a most remarkably caparisoned servant stood at attention. He wore a scarlet coat of unimaginable vividness, a cut-away coat of glaring scarlet broadcloth. But we could have passed that easily enough. The thing that held us was his blue plush knee breeches. It didn't seem fitting that a man in this age of work and wisdom should wear shimmering blue plush knee breeches for everyday. He was a big fellow and puffy. And the scarlet coat and blue breeches certainly gave the place an olden golden air. But alas! The twentieth century burst in. For he bowed us to an elevator — a modern Chicago elevator inspected by an accident company, guaranteeing the passengers against injuries! From the elevator we were emptied into a nineteenth century corridor, guarded by a twentieth century soldier and then we were turned by him into a waiting room. It was floored with marquetry, ceiled with brown and gold decoration — but modern enough — and walled in old tapestry. The room expressed the ornate impotent gorgeousness of a useless leisure class. Four or five tables, cases and stands, backed standoffishly against the tapestry on the walls, and the legs and bases of this furniture were great — unbelievably great, rococo gilded legs — legs that writhed and twisted themselves in a sheening agony of impossible forms, before they resigned themselves to dropping to the floor in distress.

Henry nudged me as our Kansas eyes bugged out at the Byzantine splendour and whispered: " Bill, what this place needs is a boss buster movement. How the Kansas legislature would wallop this splendour in the appropriation bill! How the Sixth District outfit would strip the blue plush off our upholstered friend by the elevator and

He wore a scarlet coat of unimaginable vividness, a
cutaway coat of glaring scarlet broadcloth

send him shinning home in a barrel. Topeka," sighed Henry, deeply impressed, "never will equal this!"

In this room we met a soldierly young prince, in a dark blue dress uniform, with a light blue sash across his shoulder. He shook hands with us. And he wore gloves and didn't say, "Excuse my glove," as we do in Kansas! But he was polite enough for the Grand Duke himself; indeed we thought he was the Grand Duke until we saw Medill and the minister stalking through another door, saw the minister formally bowing and then we found that we had been moved into another room — a rather plainly furnished office room, such as one might find in New York or Chicago when one called on the head of a bank or of an industrial corporation. We had left the "days of old when knights were bold," and had come bang! into the latest moment of the twentieth century. We were shaking hands rather cordially with a kindly-eyed, bald-headed little man in a grey VanDyke beard, who wore a black frock coat, rather a low-cut white vest, a black four-in-hand rather wider than the Fifth Avenue mode, striped dark grey trousers, and no jewelry except a light double-breasted gold watch-chain. He was the Duke of Genoa, who to all intents and purposes is the civilian ruler of Italy while the King is with the army. We found four chairs grouped around a sofa, and we sat while the duke, with a diffidence that amounted to shyness, talked with us about most unimportant things. The interview was purely ceremonial. It had no relation to the passports we were asking from his government to visit the Italian front, though this request had made the visit necessary. Several times there were pauses in the conversation — dead stops in the talk, which court etiquette required the Duke to repair. We didn't worry about them, for always he began to repair these gaps in the talk rather bashfully but kindly, and always the subject was impersonal and of indifferent interest. He made no sign that the interview was over, but we knew, as well as though a gong had struck, when to go. So we went, and it seemed to me that the Duke put more real enthusiasm into his good-bye than into his welcome. It was half-past five. He had been at work since eight. And perhaps it was fancy, but there seemed to be rising into his bland Italian eye a determination to knock off and take a half holiday.

We noticed that his desk was clean, as clean as General Pershing's or Major Murphy's in

Paris, or President Wilson's in Washington. Then it came to us that the king's job, after all, is a desk job. The king who used to go around ruling with a sceptre has given place to a gentleman in a business suit who probably rings for his stenographer and dictates in part as follows: "Yours of even date received and contents noted; in reply will say!" We carried away an impression that the lot of royalty, like the policeman's lot, "is not a happy one." Talking it all over, we decided that in the modern world there is really any amount more fun running a newspaper than being a king, and for the size of the town, much more chance of getting things done.

It did not fall to me because of an illness, but a few days later it fell to Henry and Medill to see a real king at Udine. He was living in a cottage a few miles out of town in a quiet little grove that protected him from airplanes. Now Henry's nearest brush to royalty was two years ago when in the New York suffrage campaign his oratory had brought him the homage of some of the rich and the great. Kings really weren't so much of a treat to Medill, who had taken his fill of them in childhood when his father was minister to England. But nevertheless they lorded it over me when they saw me because the

king wasn't on my calling list. But they
couldn't keep from me the sad fact that they had
started out to make the royal call without gloves
— hoping probably to catch the king with their
bare hands — and had been turned back by the
Italian colonel who had them in charge. Henry
once sang in the cantata of " Queen Esther," and
Medill insists that all the way up to the royal
cottage Henry kept carolling under his breath the
song: " Then go thou merrily, then go thou
merrily, unto the king!" and also: " Haman,
Haman, long live Haman, he is the favoured
one in all the king's dominions!" just to show
that finical colonel who took them back to Udine
for gloves that Wichita was no stranger to the
inside politics of the court. However, gloves
seemed to be the only ceremonial frill required,
and they went to the king's business office as in-
formally as they would go to the private room of
a soap-maker in Cincinnati. They found the king
a soft-spoken little man. Henry said he looked
very much like the mayor of Kansas City, and
was equally unassuming and considerate. He
asked his guests what had become of the Progressive party, and they pointed to themselves as the
" captain and crew of the Nancy brig." Then they
talked on for a time about many things — such as

would interest the Walrus and the Carpenter. Then the accounts of the visit changed. This is Henry's: " Well, finally after Medill began cracking his knuckles and the king began crossing and recrossing his legs, I saw it was time to go. I knew how the king felt. Every busy man has to meet a lot of bores. I sit hours with bores who flow into the Wichita *Beacon* office, and I began to appreciate just how the king felt. So I cleared my throat and said: ' Well Medill, don't you think we'd better excuse ourselves to his majesty and go? ' The king put up his hand mildly and said: ' O please! ' and the colonel in charge of the party gulped at my sympathy for the king; but I was not to be balked, and we all rose and after shaking hands around, the colonel led us out. And I didn't know that I had committed social manslaughter until the colonel exclaimed when we were in the corridor: ' Oh you republicans — you republicans, how you do like to show royalty its place! ' "

Medill has another version. He declares that Henry stood the king's obvious ennui as long as he could, then he rose and cried: " O King! live for ever, but Medill and I must pull our freight! " This version probably is apochryphal! The Italian colonel declares that Henry

expostulated: "Well, how in the dickens was I
to know that a king always gives the high sign
for company to leave!"

This Italian king is a vital institution. He
could be elected president. For he is a mixer,
in spite of his diffident ways. When the army
in Northern Italy was hammering away at the
Austrians, the king was with the soldiers. One
gets the impression that he is with the people
pretty generally in their struggle with the privileged classes. For he has lived peaceably with
a socialist cabinet for some time. He is wise
enough to realize that if the aristocracy is crumbling, the institution of royalty will crumble with
aristocracy if royalty makes an ally of the nobility. So the king and the Socialists get along
splendidly. Now the Socialists in Italy are of
several kinds. There are the city Socialists, who
are chiefly interested in industrial conditions —
wages, old age pensions, employment insurance,
and the like; a group much like the Progressive
party in the United States of 1912. We saw the
works and ways of these Socialists in every
Italian town that we visited. Either they or the
times have done wonders. And at any rate this
is the first time in Italian history when industrial
prosperity has so generally reached the workers

that they are lifted almost bodily into the middle classes. Then there are the Socialists who emphasize the land question, and they have had smaller success than their industrial brethren. We went one fine day to Frascatti by automobile. Our road took us out south of Rome over the New Appian way, through fertile acres lying in a wide beautiful plain. We passed through half a dozen little agricultural villages, mean but picturesque. None of the splendid prosperity of the cities has penetrated here. The people in these towns are peasants — and look it. They are the peasant people who live in the canvasses of the artists of the Renaissance. Half a thousand years has not changed them. Along the dusty roads we passed huge wine-carts. Two bell-bearing mules tandem gave warning to other passing carts of a cart's approach. The driver of the cart was curled up in his shaded seat asleep. The mules took their way. Carts passed and repassed each other on the road. Autos whizzed by. Still the drivers slept. They were ragged, frowsy, stupid looking. They all wore colour, one a crimson belt, another a blue shirt, a third a red handkerchief about his head. They would make better pictures than citizens, we thought. In Rome and Genoa the people would make better citizens than pictures. All day going to Frascatti and coming home we passed these beggarly looking peasant farmers. At Frascatti, which stands proudly upon a great hill overlooking the Roman plain, we saw the rich acres stretching away for miles toward Rome and beyond it. Villages flashed in the sun, white and iridescent, and the squares of vineyards and the tall Lombardy poplars made a landscape that rested the eye and soothed the soul. We stood looking at it for a long time. With us were some high officials of the Italian government.

"A wonderful landscape," said Henry to our hosts.

"In all the world there is no match for it," said Medill.

"It has lain this way for three thousand years, bearing crops year after year!" explained our host.

"Signor," said a friend of our host, "they tell me that this land yields seven per cent net."

"Yes," replied our host. "I was talking to a man in the agricultural department about it the other day; it really nets seven per cent."

"What's this land worth an acre?" This question came from me, who has the Kansas man's seven devil lust to put a price on land.

" Well — I don't —" Our host looked at his Italian friends. They gazed, puzzled and bewildered, and consulted one another. The discussion developed a curious situation. No one knew the price of that land. With us, out in the Middle West, a boy learns the probable price of the land in his neighborhood, as soon as he learns the points of the compass. Finally our host explained: " The truth of the matter is that this land never has been sold in the memory of living men. Probably most of it has remained in its present ownership for from three hundred to five hundred years. No one sells land in Italy."

And that revealed much; there was the whole program of the agrarian Socialist. The man on the wine-cart asleep, the peasant villages, the rags and the poverty, the hovels that we saw on the rich land and the crumbling aristocracy of Rome, living meanly, striving vainly, bewildered, and bedevilled, trying to make profits out of a dormant tenantry, grinding seven per cent out of the land and yet losing money by it—all these things were the meat of the answer, which recounted the long unbroken line of feudal ownership of the land. Wooden ploughs and oxen, women yoked with beasts of burden, vines and vines planted and replanted through the centuries; no capital to develop the land; insufficient profits to wake up the tenants, master and servant going gradually down in a world where labour and capital, sharing profits equitably, are rising; it was a disheartening problem.

Then in due course we left Rome and went to the Italian army on the front, and there we saw another side of the shield. From Udine in Northern Italy we journeyed into the mountains where the Italian army at that time was holding the mountain tops against the Austrians. Wherever we ascended we saw white ribbons of roads twining up the green soft mountain sides that face Italy. These roads have been made since the war. Nearly four thousand miles of them furnish approaches to the Alpine heights. They are hard-surfaced, low-graded, wide highways gouged into the mountain side. Two automobiles may pass at full speed anywhere on these roads. And all night they were alive with wagon trains bearing supplies to the front. Women help the men mend the roads. We saw few Austrian prisoners at work on the Italian roads; possibly because we were too near the front line trenches to see prisoners who are kept thirty kilos back of the line, and possibly because they have better work for the Austrians — work that old men and women cannot do. Whenever we threaded our way up a mountain side and came to a top, we found its flanks tunnelled with deep wicker-walled, broad-floored, well-drained trenches, and its top honeycombed with runways for ammunition and with great rooms for soldiers and holes for gun barrels. Mountain top after mountain top has been made into a Gibraltar by the Italians. That Gibraltar was 300 miles long, before they lost it to the Germans. But they had few guns in their fortress. They showed us emplacement after emplacement without a stick of artillery in it. They had told the French and the English of their plight, and a few artillery companies had been sent in; but only a fraction of the need. There was no central council of the allies then. Every nation was running its own little war, and Italy was left to fall, and now the four thousand miles of Italian roads, and the 300 miles of Gibraltar are German military strongholds that will have to be conquered with our blood and iron. Probably no battle line in the world today is more interesting than the Italian front was in the autumn of 1917. The south face of the Alps often is green and beautiful, but generally the northern faces of those mountains are bleak and rugged and steep.

The battle line ran a zig-zag course through the mountains, now meeting in gulches, now scurrying away up to mesas, again climbing to the top of the barren heights. We stood one sunny day on a quiet sector of the Pasubio. We were with the Liguria brigade, the 157–158th infantry. Through a peep-hole in the trench we looked across a gulch to another mountainside and saw there the Austrian trenches, not 200 yards away. Before them lay the ugly scar of brown rusted barbed wire, and just below the wire, sprawled out on the white limestone of the steep mountainside, lay fifty dead Italian soldiers who had vainly charged into the machine guns up that formidable slope. They had lain there for weeks. It was the grisliest sight we had seen during our adventures.

Medill and Henry went to another lookout, leaving me with the Italian soldiers in the trench. Their luncheon came up, a fine rich soup, with bread cubes in it, some potatoes and vegetables. It looked palatable and was good. There was enough, but not plenty. As we sat in the trench waiting for Henry and Medill, one of the heroes beside me, after thinking it all out carefully, burst forth with this:

"I livea in Pittsburgh."

It was plain to his comrades that he had put his meaning through to me. They clearly were impressed by his prowess. This cheered him up. He went on to further linguistic feats.

" Is, I live-a there five year."

That also got over and his comrades realized that he was a polyglot. Then in a joyous spirit of over-confidence, he waved the oriflamme of speech in our faces.

" Is, my papa he live-a in Brooklyn. He keepa da butcha shop and is maka da roast bif. Is, my papa's brodder he live-a in Brooklyn too. He keepa da saloon and is maka da jag! " Then we shook hands as fellow Americans.

In another hour we had wormed our way through the tunnels to the other side of the peak, and had scrambled down the mountainside to the general headquarters. Never since Hannibal's day were more interesting brigade headquarters established. They were niched into the mountain side about 4,000 feet above a gorge below. The sleeping quarters and offices were half tunnelled into the hillside. The diningroom was mounted on a platform overlooking the gorge below. Across the gorge a quarter of a mile away an aerial tram ran. That morning two airplanes — an Italian plane and an Austrian —

met out by the tram wire in a battle. It could be seen as easily from the diningroom platform as if it had been half down the block; yet the airmen were 4,000 feet in the air. We had luncheon at the brigade headquarters, and it was made a gala occasion. Some one had brought in an Austrian cow which was brigade property and we had real cream. Otherwise it was a war dinner. We had hors d'ouvres — thin sliced dried ham, sausages, and sardines — a delectable paste with parmesian cheese on it, roast beef and brown potatoes, salad and broiled chicken, and then the chef d'ouvres, the cream upon a charlotte russe! After that came cheese and coffee. Chianti and a cider champagne were served. The mess was proud of itself, as it should have been. But it seems sad to think how soon that Austrian cow went home. For within three weeks from the time we sat there, the general had surrendered in the gulch below the air-tram wire and the Germans had come with their big guns to fill the vacant emplacements!

We spent one night on our journey along the Italian front at Vicenza, and there, although the place was jammed full of soldiers, we left the war behind to stroll by moonlight over the beautiful mediaeval town. There is a fine square there — not so broad as the square at St. Mark's where the tourists used to feed the doves, but to me it seemed as beautiful.   For upon the square was the famous arcade which Palladio erected around the city-hall of the place.   It stood beautiful and gloomy before us in the moonlight, one of the world's real bits of architecture.   As Americans we had a special interest in the arcade because it was typical of the best of Palladio's work and our own Thomas Jefferson, studying it, had reproduced it and Americanized it in some of the buildings of the University of Virginia, buildings that have had a distinct influence upon American architecture!   A number of Palladio's other works we saw that night, softened and glorified by the moonlight.   And we saw also an old French house, not twenty-five feet wide, but a gem of French architecture erected before the discovery of America.   Finally we went back and stood by the statue of Palladio and listened to the low rumble of the guns on the front and wondered what the Germans would do with such a lovely thing as this Vicenza if by any chance they ever took it.   That day we had looked down from a mountain-top upon an Austrian town lying peacefully in the valley below us directly under the Italian guns.   The guns of the Austrians and the Italians were smashing away at each other from the mountain-tops over and across the town.

" You could pulverize that town easily enough," Henry said to the Italian who was taking the Americans through the trenches.

" Oh, yes," he answered.   " But it's a beautiful little town! Why ruin it? " His theory was that if the Italians took it they would want it whole and would want the loyalty and respect of the people of the town; if they did not take it, why smash a beautiful little town just to be smashing?

The German theory, of course, is exactly opposite to this. They would smash the town, if they were to take it, to put fear into the hearts of the inhabitants and command obedience; and if they knew they could not take it they would smash it to cripple the enemy that much! We of the Allies desire respect and loyalty that come from reason. The Germans demand unreasoning obedience and denied that, they destroy. One philosophy is Christian; the other Babylonian. But the devilish strength of the German philosophy came to us more forcibly in Italy than it came elsewhere because of certain contrasts. They were contrasts in what might be called public wisdom. The Germans take better care of their poor than some of the Allies. The Germans know that poverty is a curse to a nation, and during the past generation they have done much to alleviate it. And in alleviating poverty they have kept their poor docile; and they go into battle feeling that they have something to fight for. In the allied countries too often we have let the devil take the hindermost. As we rode one afternoon from Vicenza to Milan we wondered, looking at the farms and the farmers along the road, why those farmers should be asked to die for a country that kept them in so low an estate. And yet they were better off than the farmers of Southern Italy. But in socializing industry the Italian farmer has been forgotten, and when the press came upon the Italian front, thousands of ignorant peasant soldiers lay down their arms, deluded by a German spy ruse so simple that it should have fooled no intelligent soldier. But they were not intelligent. Their intelligence had been eaten up by their landlords for generations, and in a crisis the German civilization overcame its enemy! You cannot shake the sleeping peasant on the wine-cart from a thousand years' sleep and make him get up and go out and whip a soldier who is even half awake!

As we rode from Vicenza to Milan we had a curious experience. There entered our compartment at twilight one of the carabinieri! We had been looking with admiration at the carabinieri for days. They were well-set-up soldiers, apparently of a picked grade of men, who wore wide cocked hats, like those worn by the British troops in the American revolution. The cocked hats of the Italian carabinieri are as wide as their handsome shoulders and they make striking figures. This one who entered our compartment was drunk — grandly, gorgeously and sociably drunk. He wanted to talk to us. He tried Italian and we shook our heads. Then Medill tackled him in French and he shook his head. Then Henry squared off and gave him the native Kansas English — with appropriate gestures. But the Italian sighed amiably and it was clear he was balked. Then he looked up and down the outer corridor of the car, came in, shut the door and smiled as broadly as his cocked hat.

"Sprecken sie Deutsch?" he asked, and Medill answered, "Seemlich!" When it was apparent that two of us understood German he opened up. He had to talk slowly, but he was willing to make any sacrifice to get conversation going. He rambled along in a maudlin way, and finally picked up an illustrated paper containing an account of the Turin riots, which angered him, and then and there being, that Italian soldier told us in German the story of what he called der grosser rebellion! To talk German in an allied country today is as much as one's life is worth. For a soldier to talk German is a crime; for a soldier to tell three foreigners about a riot in his country, which he, as a soldier behind machine guns had to suppress, killing hundreds, was mighty near to treason. And we gasped. We thought he might be testing us out as potential spies. So we shut up. But he ambled on, and slowly, as the liquor overcame him, he ran down and went sound asleep with the offending paper in his arms. Perhaps he was one of those Germans wearing the Italian uniform who in the German drive three weeks later gave commands to the ignorant peasant regiments to lay down their arms and surrender! At least it was reported in Europe that thousands of them abandoned their works under the command of German spies!

When we arrived at Milan we found there waiting for us a note from the Gilded Youth, whom we had met coming over on the boat from America. And it brought back our everlasting love affair. It is curious how that love affair kept projecting itself into the consciousness of two middle-aged men who reasonably may be supposed to have passed out of the zone of true romance. But the memory of the hazel eyes of the Gilded Youth as he gazed at the pretty face of the young nurse there in the moonlight at Landrecourt, with such exaltation and joy, kept bobbing back into our minds as we saw other lovers in other lands, married and single, crossing our paths. And there was the Young Doctor, diffident and reticent, who had his heart set on the girl, and the contest furnished us with a death-less theme for speculation. And here at Milan came this letter — just a note forwarded from Paris — telling us that the Gilded Youth could " stand and wait " no longer; he was going to hit back. He had quit the Ambulance service for aviation. And he was in a training camp near Paris. We wondered how many times during his training he would slip across the sky to Landrecourt to visit his true love. The one-horse buggy had been the only lover's chariot known to Henry and me, and we remembered how a red-wheeled cart used to lay out the neigh-bours in the heroic days of the nineties. So in our meditative moments we considered what a paralysing spectacle it would be for the neigh-

We thought he might be testing us out as potential
spies

bours to see a young man come swooping down
upon his lady love's bower in an airplane and
Henry, who was betting on the Gilded Youth as
against the Doctor, began taking even money
again!

Milan we found today is an industrial town,
entirely modern, dominated not by the cathedral as of old, but by the spirit of the new Italy.
They took us to a luncheon given by the American
chamber of commerce. We heard nothing of
their antiquities, and little of their ruins. We
had to fight to get time to see the cathedral,
whose windows are boarded up or filled with
white glass; but the Milanese were anxious to
have us see their great factories; their automobile
works, their Caproni airship plant and the up-
to-the-minute organization of industrial efficiency
everywhere. Here in Milan we saw thousands
of men out of uniform, but wearing the rib-
bon arm-band of the industrial reservists. We
fancied these Milanese were bigger, huskier men
than the men in the south of Italy, and that they
looked better-kept and better-bred. They certainly are a fierce and indomitable people. The
Austrians don't raid the Milanese in airships.
They said that once the Austrians came and the
next day the Milanese loaded up a fleet of big

Capronis with 30,000 pounds of high explosives, sailed over Austria and blew some town to atoms. So Milan has never been bothered since as other border towns of Italy have been bothered by air-raiders. The days we spent in Milan were like days in a modern American industrial city — say Toledo, or St. Paul or Detroit or Kansas City.

Turin is similarly modern and industrial, though not so beautiful as Milan. In Turin we saw the scene of the riot — the " grosser rebellion," which our carabinieri friend told us about. Signor Nitti, now a member of the Italian cabinet, who entertained us in Rome, told the Italian parliament — according to the American newspapers — that the millers caused the riot. The bread ration did not come to Turin one morning, and the working people struck. Nitti says the millers were hoarding flour and caused the delay. The strike grew general over the city. Workers wandering about the town were threatened with the police if they congregated. They congregated, and some troops from a nearby training camp were called. The troops were new; they were also friends of the strikers. They refused to fire. Then the strikers built barricades in the streets and in a day or so the regular troops came down from the mountains with machine guns, fired on the barricades and when hundreds were hit the rebellion was quelled.   And Signor Nitti says it was all because some profit hog stopped the ordinary flow of flour from the farmer to the consumer of bread!   There is, of course, the other side.   They told us in Turin that boys in their teens were found dead back of the barricades with thousand lire notes in their pockets, and that German agents came during the first hours of the strike and spread money lavishly to make the riot a rebellion.   Probably this is true.   The profiteer made the strike possible.   It was an opportunity for rebellion, and Germany took the opportunity.   Always she is on hand with spies to buy what she cannot honestly win.

Reluctantly we turned our faces from Italy to France.   Yet the journey had been well worth while.   We came home with a definite and hopeful impression about Italy.   The Turin riot, bad as it was, was not an anti-war riot.   It was directed at the bad administration of the food controller.   Italy then was not an invaded country, as France was, and had no such enthusiasm for the war, as a nation has when its soil is invaded. Italy has that enthusiasm now for the war.   We saw that her man-power was hardly tapped.   She has millions to pour into the trenches. She needs and will need until the end of the war, iron and coal. She will have to borrow her guns and her fuel. But she has almost enough food. We found sugar scarce; butter scarce, and bread sharply allowanced in hotels and restaurants. We found two meatless days a week besides Friday and found the people, as a rule, observing them. We found the industries of the nation turned solely toward the war. Italy realizes what defeat means. The pro-Austrian party which was strong at the beginning of the war has vanished, and since the invasion, even the Pope has lost his interest in peace!

But all these things are temporary; with the war's passing they will pass. The real thing we found was an awakening people, coming into the new century eager and wise and sure that it held somewhere in its coming years the dawn of a new day. That really is the hope of the war — an industrial hope, not a political hope, not a geographical hope, but a hope for better things for the common man. It is a hope that Christianity may take Christendom, and that the fellowship among the nations of the world so devoutly hoped for, may be possible because of a fellowship among men inside of nations.

CHAPTER VII

WHEREIN WE CONSIDER THE WOMAN
PROPOSITION

IT is curious how the human heart throws out homeseeking tendrils. As we crossed the Italian frontier and came back into France, keen longing for the Ritz — even the Ritz with its gloomy grandeur came to me, and Henry confessed that he was glad to get back to a country where a man could get a good refreshing bowl of onion soup! After dinner, our first evening at the Ritz, we were looking over the theatrical offerings advertised upon the wall by the elevator at the hotel, when whom should we meet but "Auntie," the patrician relative of the Gilded Youth. She recognized us in our civilian clothes, and it fell to me to make the fool blunder of complicating our formal greetings with gaiety. Auntie's troubled face would have caught Henry's quick sensitive eyes. But Auntie's voice brushed aside the levity of the opening.

"Haven't you heard — haven't you heard?" she asked. And we knew instinctively that something had happened to the Gilded Youth. And when one is in aviation something happening always is serious. It was Henry's kind voice that conveyed our sympathy to her. And she told us of the accident. Two mornings before, while making his first flight alone, from the training camp near Paris, something went wrong with his engine while he was but a thousand feet in the air — and over Neuilly. He had to glide down, and being over a town he could not make a landing. They took him from the wreck of his plane, to the hospital near by — fortunately an American Red Cross Hospital, where the people recognized him and sent for his aunt. All day and all night he had lain unconscious, and at noon had opened his eyes for a minute to find his aunt beside him. "I brought with me," said Auntie, in a tone so significantly casual that it arrested our attention before she added, "that capable young nurse, the first assistant —" As she spoke she caught Henry's eyes and held him from looking at me.

"You mean the one —" said Henry in a tone quite as casual as Auntie's while giving eye for eye.

"Yes, your pretty mid-western girl. She is with him now." Then Auntie lost Henry's eyes as tears brimmed into her own. " It has been twenty-six hours since we arrived at Neuilly. I shall return in an hour, and —"

" I wish," cried Henry, " I wish there was something we could do! "

Auntie caught our embarrassed desire to be of service yet not to assume. Her strong fine face lighted with something kind enough for a smile, as she answered: " Couldn't you go out and see him? I think no one else in Paris would be more welcome than you two! "

That puzzled us. She saw us looking our question at each other, and went on: " Life means more to him now than it ever has meant." She really smiled as she quoted: " ' It means intensely and it means good! ' " Auntie's tired eyes gathered us in again. " When you left Landrecourt last month he told me much about the voyage over here on the *Espagne*." The tired eyes left us to follow the crippled elevator boy who went pegging down the corridor as she continued: " about his days in Paris before he went back to his ambulance unit; about his meeting you that night near Douaumont,— at the first aid post and — and I know," she paused a second, pulled herself together and continued gently. " We must face things as they are. The boy's hours in this earth are short. He has other friends here, of course — old friends, but you —" again she stopped. "You will appreciate why when you see him."

So we gave up the poor travesty upon life that we should have seen behind the footlights for a glimpse into one of life's real dramas.

It was nearly midnight before we came to Neuilly and stood awkwardly beside the white cot in the little white room where the Gilded Youth was lying. How the gilding had fallen off! All white and broken he lay, a crushed wreck of a man, with the cluttering contrivances of science swathing him, binding him, encasing him, holding him miserably together while the tide of life ran out. But when he wakened he could smile. There was real gilding in that smile, the gilding of youth, but he only flashed his eyes upon us for a fleeting second in turning his smile to her — to the Eager Soul, to her who had brought some new incandescence into his life. Then we knew why his aunt had said that we should see him. He would have us who had witnessed the planting of the seed, know how it had flowered. His smile told us that also. He could lift no hand to us, and could speak but faintly. Yet his greeting held something princely in it —

fine and sweet and brave. Then he did a curious thing. He began whistling very softly under his breath and between his teeth a queer little tune, that reminded one oddly of the theme of Tschaicovski's Symphony Pathétique — the first movement. As he whistled he turned from Henry and me and looked at the Eager Soul, who smiled back intelligently, and when she smiled he stopped. We could not understand their signals. But whatever it was so far as it pretended to a show of courage, we knew that it was a gorgeous bluff. In the fleeting glance that he gave us, he told us the truth; and we knew that he was pretending to the others that he did not know. We made some cheerful nothings in our talk, and would have gone but he held us. The Eager Soul looked at her watch, gave him some medicine, which we took to be a heart stimulant; for he revived under it, and said to me:

"Remember — that night at Douaumont?"

"Where you whistled the 'Meditation from Thais,' in the moonlight?"

"Yes," he murmured, "and we — watched — the trucks — come out of the mist — full of life — and go into the mist,— toward death."

"Wonderful — wasn't it!" sighed one of us.

"Symbolic," he whispered. And our eyes followed his to the vivid face of the Eager Soul, in the halo of her nurse's cap. She was exceedingly glorious, and animate and beautiful. And he was passing into the mist, out toward death. He saw that he had got the figure to me, and smiled. Then suddenly something came into his face from afar, and he seemed to know that his frail craft had mounted the out-going tide. Slowly, very slowly life began to fade from his face. Further and further from shore the tide was bearing him. We seemed to be on the pier. The Eager Soul even leaned forward and put out a pretty hand, and waved at him. He signalled back with a twitch of his lips that was meant for a smile. And then we at the pier lost the last gleam of life and saw only the broken bark, wearily riding the racing tide.

And then we turned from the pier and went our several ways back into the midst of life. We were going home, and getting ready to go home is a joyous proceeding. And there was another significance to our packing to leave Paris. It meant something more than a homeward journey; it meant that for the first time since we left Wichita and Emporia in midsummer we were turning our backs on war. It took a tug to make the turn. From all over the earth the

war draws men to it like an insatiable whirl-
pool. And as we came nearer and nearer to war
we had felt it swallow men into its vortex — men,
customs, institutions, civilizations, indeed the age
and epoch wherein we lived, we had felt moving
into chaos — into nothing, to be reborn some day
into we know not what, in the cataclysm out
there on the front. We had seen it. But seeing
it had revealed nothing. For many nights we
had heard the distant roar of the hungry guns
ever clamouring for more food, for the blood of
youth, for the dreams of age, for the hopes of a
race, for the creed of an era. And we left them
still ravening, mad and unsated. And we were
going away as dazed as we were when we came.
But as we packed our things in Paris, the thrall
of it still gripped us and the consciousness that
we were leaving the war was as strong in our
hearts as the joy we felt at turning homeward.
But we got aboard the train and rode during the
long lovely morning down the wide rich valley
of the Seine, past Rouen, through Normandy
with its steep hills which seem reflected in the
sharp peaked roofs of its châteaux, and through
musty mediaeval towns, in which it was hard to
realize that modern industry was hiving. The
hum of industry seemed badly out of key in a

town with a cathedral whose architectural roots are a thousand years old, and whose streets have not yet been veined with sewers, and whose walls are gay with the façades of the fifteenth century. The whole face of the landscape, town and country side, seemed to us like the back drop of the first act in a comic opera, and we were forever listening for " The Chimes of Normandy! " Instead we heard the noon whistle. It was tremendously incongruous. How American humour cracks into sardonic ribaldry at the spectacle. The French are the least bit unhappy about this American humour. They don't entirely see it. Once outside of a poor French village near the war zone, that had been bombed from the German lines, bombed from the German airships and ravaged by fire and sword, some American soldiers, looking at the desolation and the ruin of the place, so grotesque in its gaping death, so hopeless in its pitiful finality, painted on a large white board, and nailed on a sign post just at the edge of the town this slogan:

" Watch Commercy Grow! Boost for the Old Town! "

But in that flash of humour the tragedy of Commercy stood revealed clearer than in a flood of tears!

We came at the end of the morning "to a port in France." From there we were to take the boat for England. And it seemed to us that the whole place was bent on the same errand. English soldiers going home on leave jammed the streets. They filled the hotels; they crowded into the shops. And the whole town was made over for them. "French Spoken Here" was the facetious sign someone had stuck on a postcard shop near the grey old church on the main thoroughfare. It is curious how the English put their trade mark upon the places they occupy. These French ports filled with British soldiers look more English than England. The English demand their own cooking, their own merchandise, their own tobacco, their own beer — which is stale, flat and unprofitable enough these days — and they demand their native speech. When he gets in sight of his native land the British Tommy quits saying "Donny mo-i, de tabac! Ma'mselle!" But bellows forth both loud and long, "I say, Lizz, gimme some makin's! and look alive, please!" So when we went to bed in our boat in a French port, and slept through a submarine zone, and waked up in an English port, there was no vast difference in the places. Today Southampton and Dover are much like Calais and Havre; for there the English do most congregate. But back of the French ports it is all France, and back of the English ports is England, and worlds lie between them. England, as one rides through it who lives beyond the seas, and uses the English tongue, always must seem like the unfolding of an old, old dream. England gives her step-children the impression that they have seen it all before! And they have; in Mother Goose, in Dickens, in Shakespeare, in Thackeray, in Trollope, in the songs of British poets, in the landscapes of British artists! At every turn of the road, in every face at the window, in every hedgerow and rural village is the everlasting reminder that we who speak the English tongue are bound with indissoluble links of our foster memories from the books and the arts, to ways of thinking and living and growing in grace that we call English. It is more than a blood or breed, more even than a civilization, is this spiritual inheritance that comes from this English soil; it is the realization in life of a philosophy, the dramatization of a human creed. It may be understood, but not defined, yet it is as palpable and substantial in this earth as any material fact. Germany knows what this English philosophy means; and for half a century Germany has been preparing to combat it.   Napoleon knew it, and believed in it, when he declared three-fourths of every fact is its spiritual value.   France has it, new Russia is struggling for it.   American life has it as an ancient inheritance, and as we Americans rode through the green meadows of England up from the coast to London, for ever reviewing familiar scenes and faces and aspects of life that we had never seen before, we realized how much closer than blood or geography or politics men grow who hold the same creed.   So Henry, feeling that restraints no longer were necessary when we were as near home as England, began fussing with an Englishman about something a speaker had said in parliament the day before.   We may love the French, like the ladies, God bless 'em!   But we quarrel only with the English.

When we came to London we saw, even as we whirled through the grey old streets, surface differences between London and the other capitals of the Allies, so striking that they were marked contrasts.   These differences marked the different reactions of personal loss upon the different nations.   France expresses her loss in mourning; she relieves her emotions in visible grief.   Italy does this also; but her losses have been smaller than the French losses and Italy's sorrow is less in evidence than is the woe of France. But England's master passion in this war is pride. " In proud and loving memory " is a phrase that one sees a hundred times every day in the obituary notices of those who have died for England. Ambassador Page tells this: He was asking a British matron about her family, severally, and when he inquired about the son, she replied, " Haven't you heard of the new honour that has come to us through him? " And to her friend's negative she returned: " He has been called upon to die for England! " Now that seems rather French in its dramatics than British. Yet it reflects exactly the British attitude. The women wear no mourning. They do not go about in bright colours by any means. Bright colours in the war distinguish the men. But the women do wear dark blues, lavenders and purples, dark wine colours and neutral tints of various hues. The shop windows of London are bright. There is a faint re-echo of the time when Great Britain said, " Business as usual." The busy life, the shopping crowds, the street throngs, and the heavy streams of trade that flow through the highways of London, prove that London still is a great city — the greatest city in the world; and even the war, black and dread and horrible as it is, cannot overcome London, entirely. Something of the fact that she is the world's metropolis, more permanent than the war, somewhat apart from the war, and indeed above it, still lingers in the London consciousness, however remotely.

One must not imagine that London is unchanged. It is greatly changed, for the men are gone. One sees fewer men in London out of uniform than in Paris. And the Londoners one does see, all appear to be hurrying about war work. But it is the women constantly in evidence who have changed the face of London. Women keep the shops, conduct the busses, run the street cars, drive the trucks, sit on the seats of the horse-drays, deliver freight, manage railway trains, sweep the streets, wait on the tables, pull elevator ropes, smash baggage at the railway stations, sell tickets, usher at the theaters, superintend factories, make munitions, lift great burdens before forges, plough, reap, and stack grain and grass on farms, herd sheep in waste places, hew wood and draw water, and do all of the world's work that man has ever done. Now, of course, women are doing these things elsewhere in the world. But London and England are man's domain. It seems natural to see the French women, and even the Italian women at work. Man is more or less the leisure class on the continent. But London is a man's town if on earth there is one, and to see women everywhere in London is a curious and baffling sight.

Of course the men are not all dead —" they're just away." And they come back on leave. But life is not normal. War is abnormal, and there is an ever-urging desire of life to assume its normal function. So all over Europe we heard whispers about the moral break-down among the women of England. In England we were asked about the dreadful things that were happening in France. The things that were happening in France were not essentially evil things. One could imagine that if God thinks war is necessary for the solution of the world's terrible problems, He will have no trouble forgiving these lapses that follow in the wake of war in France. And in England, similarly we found that the moral break-down was not a moral break-down at all. The abnormal relation of the sexes arising out of war produced somewhat the same results that one found in France, but in different ways. In France too many strange men are billeted in the houses of the people. In England, too many homes are without men at all. And sheer social lonesomeness produces in humanity about the same conditions that arise when people are thrown in too close contact. There is a sort of social balance of nature, wherein normally desirable results are found. The girl working in the munition factories, working at top speed eight hours a day, filled with a big emotional desire to do her full duty to her country every second of the day, finds it easy in her eight hours of rest to fall in love with a soldier who is going out to offer his life for the country for which she is giving her strength so gladly. She is not a light woman. She is moved by deep and beautiful emotions. And if a marriage before he goes out to fight is inconvenient or impossible — the war made it so, and God will understand. Of course the idle woman, the vain woman, the foolish woman in these times in England finds ample excuse for her folly and vast opportunity to indulge her folly in the social turmoil of the war. And she is going the pace. Her men are gone, who restrain her, and she has nothing in her head or her heart to hold, and she is in evidence. Her type always exaggerates its importance, and fools people into thinking that her name is Legion, and that Mr. Legion is an extensive polygamist, with a raft of daughters and sisters and cousins and aunts. But she is small in numbers and she is not important. She is merely conspicuous, and the moral break-down in England, that one hears of in the baited breath of the continent, is an illusion.

The elevator girl at Bucklands Hotel in London was a bright, black-eyed, good looking woman in her late twenties. She wore a green uniform with a crimson voile boudoir cap and as the American stepped inside the slow-going car, she answered his " good morning " with a respectful, " good morning, sir." Being a good traveller, it seemed to me wise to prepare to while away the tedium of the long easy journey to the fourth floor with a friendly chat.

" Any of your relatives in the war? " This from me by way of an ice-breaker.

" Yes, sir, my husband, sir," she replied as she grasped the cable. She gave it a pull, and added "— or he was, sir. He's home now, sir! "

" On leave? "

" O no, sir, he's wounded, sir — he lost his left arm at the shoulder, sir, and he's going down to Roehampton today, sir, to see if they can teach him some kind of a trade there, sir," answered the woman.

The wonders of Roehampton where they re-educate the cripples of war and turn them out equipped with such trades as their maimed bodies may acquire had been displayed for Henry and me the day before.

"Tell him to try typewriting and stenography, one armed men are doing wonders with that down at Roehampton. Any children?"

"Two, sir," she answered as the elevator approached the mezzanine floor, "three and five, sir!"

"Three and five — well, well, isn't that fine! Aren't you lucky! Tell him to try that stenography; that will put him in an office and he'll have a fine chance to rise there. You must give them an education — a good one; send them to College. If they're going to get on in this new world they will need every ounce of education you can stuff into them. But it will be a splendid thing for both of you working for that. Is education expensive in England?"

"Very, sir. I hardly see how we can do it, sir!"

"That's too bad — now in our country education, from the primer to the university, is absolutely free. The state does the whole business and in my state they print the school books, and more than that they give a man a professional education, too, without tuition fees — if he wants to become a lawyer or a doctor or an engineer or a chemist or a school teacher!"

"Is that so, sir," the cable was running through her hands as she spoke. Then she added as the elevator passed the second floor, "If we could only have that here, sir. If we only could, sir!"

"Well, it will come. That's the next revolution you want to start when you women get the ballot. Abolish these class schools like Eton and Harrow and put the money into better board schools. All the kids in my town, and in my state, and in my whole section of the country go to the common schools. Children should start life as equals. There is no snobbery so cruel as the snobbery that marks off childhood into classes! When you women vote here, the first thing to do is to smash that nonsense. But in the meantime keep the kids in school."

"We've talked that all over," she answered. "And we're certainly going to try. He'll have his pension, and I'll have this job and he'll learn a trade and I think we can manage, sir!" The "sir" came belated.

"Go to it, sister, and luck to you," cried her passenger as he rose from his bench. The car was nearing the fourth floor.

"We shall," she answered; "no fear of that."

She stopped the car, and they smiled as friends as she let him out of the door. " Well — good morning," she said as he turned down the corridor. The " sir " had left entirely when they reached the fourth floor. And all the women of Europe, excepting perhaps those still behind the harem curtains in Turkey and Germany of whom we know nothing, are dropping the servile " sir " and are emerging into life at the fourth floor as human beings.

It may be well to digress a moment in this narrative, from our purely martial adventure, that we may consider for a few pages the woman question as it is affected by the war. To me, if not to Henry, who is highly practical, it seemed that in France and Italy, but particularly in England, the new Heaven and the new earth that is forming during this war, has created a new woman. Indeed the European woman of the war is almost American in her liberty.

" European women," said a former American grand dame of the old order, sipping tea with me at an embassy in the dim lit gorgeousness of a mediaeval room, " are of two kinds: Those who are being crucified by the war, and those who are abusing the new found liberties which war has brought them! "

" Liberties? " asked her colloquitor; not Henry. He had no patience with these theoretical excursions into speculative realms. " Liberties rather than privileges? "

" Yes, liberties. Privileges are temporary," purred the lady at the embassy. " They come and go, but the whole trouble with this new situation is that it is permanent. That also is part of the crucifixion of those who suffer under it. These women never again can return to the lives they have left, to the sheltering positions from which the awful needs of this war have driven them. The cultivated European woman, who I think on the whole was the highest product of our civilization, has gone. She has fallen to the American level."

" And the continental mistress system," prodded her American interviewer, ironically, " will it, too, disappear with the departed superiority of continental womanhood? "

" Yes, the mistress system too — if you want to call it a system — and I suppose it is an institution — it too will become degraded and Americanized."

" Americanized? " the middle western eyebrows went up, and possibly the middle western voice flinched a little. But the wise dowager from Bridgeport, Connecticut, living in Paris on New York Central bonds, continued bitterly: " Yes, Americanized and vulgarized. The continental mistress system is not the nasty arrangement that you middle class Americans think it is. Of course there are European men who acquire one woman after another, live with her a few months or a few years and forget her. Such men are impossible."

She waved away the whole lady-chasing tribe with a contemptuous hand.

" But the mistress system as we know it in Europe is the by-product of a leisure class. Men and women marry for business reasons. The women have their children to love, the man finds his mistress, and clings to her for a lifetime. He cannot afford to marry her — even if he could be divorced; for he would have to work to support her, and be declassed. But he can support her on his wife's money and a beautiful lifelong friendship is thus cherished. It will disappear when men have to work, and when women may go into the world to work without losing their social positions. And this new order, this making the world safe for democracy, as you call it, will rob civilization of its most perfect flower — the cultivated woman who has developed under the shelter of our economic system. I might as well shock your bourgeois morals now as later. So listen to this. Here is one of the ways the women of Europe are suffering. I talked to a French mother this morning. Her income is gone — part of it taxed away, and the rest of it wiped away by the Germans in Northern France. Her son has only a second lieutenant's income. In this chaos she can find no suitable wife for him. One who is rich today, tomorrow may be poor, so the dear fellow may not marry. And he is looking for a mistress, and his mother fears he will pick up a fool; for only a fool would take him on a lieutenant's salary. And the weeping mother told me she would almost as soon that her son should have no mistress as to have a fool! For a man's mistress does make such a difference in his life! My friend is almost willing to let him marry some bright poor girl and go to work! The world never will know the suffering the women of Europe are enduring in this war!"

Now we may switch off that record with the snort of woe which Henry gave when he heard it. He was trying to tell a Duchess about prohibition in Kansas, who had never heard of either Kansas or prohibition and who was clearly scandalized at what she heard of both. But

Henry's other ear was open to what the embassy ornament was saying to me. On the other side of this record of the swan song of the lady of the embassy is this record. It is a man's voice. The man has risen from an American farm, hustled his way into a place where as manager of the London factory of an American concern, he works several hundred employés.

"Say, let me tell you something — never again! Never again for mine do the men come back into our shop. We may let a dozen or so of 'em back to handle the big machines. But the next size, which we thought that only men could handle — never again. And when they come back these men will have to work under women foremen. We thought when the war took our men bosses away that we should have to close the shop. But say — never again, I tell you. And let me give you a pointer. You wouldn't know them girls. When the war broke out they were getting ten shillings — about $2.50 a week, the best of 'em, and they were mean and slovenly and kind of skinny and dirty, and every once in awhile one would drop out, and the other girls had a great joke about her — you know. And they would soak the shop whenever they got a chance! The boss had to keep right after 'em, or they'd soldier on the job or break a machine, or slight the product, and they'd lie — why, man, the whole works would stand up and lie for each other against the shop. It took five men to boss them where we have one woman doing it now. And say, it ain't the woman boss that's done it. We pay 'em more. Them same girls is getting ten and twelve and fifteen bucks a week now — Lawsee, man — you ought to see 'em! Dressed up to kill; fat, cheerful, wide-awake! Goddle-mighty, man, you wouldn't know 'em for that same measly bunch of grouches we had three years ago. And they work for the shop now, and not against it. They're different girls. I wouldn't-a believed ten dollars a week would-a turned the trick; but it's sure done it."

" Perhaps," suggested his acquaintance, " the girls are cheerful and competent because they aren't afraid of poverty. Maybe they are motived by hope of getting on in the world and not motived by the terror of slipping down. Does that not make them stand by the shop instead of working against it? Isn't it a developed middle class feeling that accepts the shop as ' their kind of people ' now? "

" Search me, Cap — I give it up. I just only know what I know and see what I see. And never again — you hear me, man — never again does our shop go back to men. The ten or twelve dollar skirt has made a hit with me! Have a cigarette?"

The net gain of women in this war, all over the world is, of course, a gain in fellowship.

But after all fellowship will be futile if it does not bear fruit. And the first fruit of the fellowship between men and women in Europe surely will be a wider and deeper influence of women upon the destinies of the European world. And who can doubt who knows woman, that her influence will be thrown first and heaviest toward a just and lasting peace.

Often while we were in London, during the last days of our stay, when the meaning of the war gradually was forming in our minds we talked of these things. There are two Henrys — one, the owner of a ten-story building in Wichita, the editor of a powerful and profitable newspaper; the other a protagonist, a sentimental idealist. To me this was his greatest charm — this infinite variety of Henrys that was forever turning up in our discourse. The owner of the Beacon building and the publisher of the newspaper had small use for my theories about the importance of the rise of woman into fellowship with men in the new democratization of the world. He refused to see the democratization of the world in the war. To him the war meant adjustment of boundaries, economic advantages, and realignments of political and commercial influence on the map of the world. But to the other Henry, to the crusader whom I had seen many times setting out on the quest for the grail in politics, throwing away his political fortunes for a cause and a creed as lightly as a man would toss aside a cigar stub, the war began to mean something more than its military expression.

And one night as we sat in our room waiting for dinner a letter came up from the Eager Soul, with some trinkets she had sent over to us by messenger to take to her mother in Denver. After telling us the news of the hospital, and of Auntie and of the wound in the Young Doctor's hand, she wrote:

" O how I hate war — hate it — hate it! And this war of all wars, I hate it worst. It is so ruthless, so inexorably cruel; so utterly meaningless, viewed at close range. Yesterday they brought me into Northern France, and I spent the twilight last night looking over the ruins of the local church. It is the most important small church in Northern France and contains one of the earliest ribbed vaults in France, they say. It was built about 1100, and now the thing is smashed. It is what our artillerymen call a one-shot church. O the waste of it — churches, men, homes, creeds! How many one-shot creeds have perished in this hell-fire! Still out of the old I suppose the new will come. But I have talked to women, to peasant women in their homes, to noble women in hospitals; to women in their shops and women on the farms, and I know that if the new world brings them as its heritage, only the enlarged comradeship they are taking with men in this time of suffering, then one thing is sure: We women will strike an awful blow at future wars! The womanhood of the past, someway, is like these sad, broken churches of France. It is shattered and gone, and in its ruins we see its exquisite beauty, its ineffable grace, its symbolism of a faith that once sufficed. But it will not be restored. We shall build new temples; we shall know new women. The old had to go, that the new might come. And our new women and our new temples shall be dedicated, not merely to faith, not merely to beauty, not merely to adoration but to service, to service and comradeship in the world."

As he finished reading the letter Henry's eyes

glistened. Its emotion had awakened the crusader, who said gently: "Well, Bill, I presume it is the potential mother in every woman that makes her worth while. And if this war will only harness motherhood to the public conscience, the net gain will be worth the war, however it is settled."

CHAPTER VIII

IN WHICH WE DISCOVER "A NEW HEAVEN AND A NEW EARTH"

FINALLY our talk left the war and its meaning, and we fell to wondering how the Young Doctor's hand was coming on, and we thought of the Eager Soul, too, standing so wistfully between love and death and the picture of the Young Doctor sitting in the garden among the flowers of early autumn, more poet than soldier or doctor, came to both of us as we talked and then Henry stooped to the floor and picked up two folded sheets of paper. Clearly they had dropped from the envelope sent to us by the Eager Soul. He opened one and remarked:

"Why, Bill, it's poetry. She's written here on the margin, 'Verses by our Doctor friend. I thought you'd like to see them. See other sheet for melody to suit. It was the melody he tried to whistle that night. He wrote them for me to fit the Doctor's words.' " Then Henry unfolded the other sheet; and there, sure enough, was the air, evidently copied by the girl from the melody written by the Gilded Youth. And clearly it was the theme of the Tschaicovski melody from the first movement of the Sixth Symphony, that dominated the air.[1] The fine thoroughbred nerve of him, trying to signal that air back to her, and to play the game of courage to us! Henry read the verses; they were headed " A Soldier's Song." They were very much such rhymes as we wrote when we were young. They ran:

Love, though these hands, that rest in thine so dear,
Back into dust may crumble with the year;
Love, though these lips, that meet thy lips so true,
Soon may be grass that stores the morning dew —
O Love, know well, that this fond heart of mine,
   It shall be always, always — thine!

Love, though our dreams shall have no hope but this;
Love, though our faith shall be our rarest bliss;
Love, though the years may bring their death and chill,
Love, though our blood shall lose its passion, still —
Still, Love, know well that this heart is divine,
   It shall be always — always, thine!

[1] For the melody which the Gilded Youth wrote to the Young Doctor's verses the reader should see appendix " A."

Henry sat holding the sheet and looking through the wall of the room in Buckland's hotel across twenty years, down an elm-shaded path in the little town of Baldwin, Kansas — thousands of miles and seemingly thousands of years away!

"Well," he sighed. "In the note here she's got her he's badly mixed. But we know what she means. And I don't blame them; any boy in his twenties ought to go singing, with one voice or another, after such a girl!"

And then we knew what the Young Doctor was doing there in the garden among the adoring flowers. He was writing those verses. And, we in our forties, after such things have passed, were sitting in a commonplace room in a comfortable hotel, five hundred miles from the battle and twenty years from the primrose path, trying to imagine it all. And like Stephen Blackpool in Dickens' "Hard Times" about all we could make of it was that it was a mess! They were both so remote, the love affair that had followed us over Europe, and the war which we had followed so wearily. The love affair was of course a look backward, for us, to days "when lutes were touched and songs were sung"; but the war and all its significance stretched ahead. It portended change. For change always follows war.

Yet life, in spite of the current of war twisting so many things askew, does proceed in England calmly, and in something like order. As we looked back upon our London experience it seemed to Henry and me that we were hurrying from luncheons to teas and teas to dinners and from dinners to the second act of good shows all the time. For in London we had no Red Cross duties. We were on our way home, and people were kind to us, and best of all we could speak the language — after a fashion — and understand in a general way what was going on. We had dined at two American embassies on the continent and had worn our tail coats. Of course Red Cross uniforms were proper evening regalia at any social function. But someway a flannel shirt and a four-in-hand tie — even a khaki coloured tie, did not seem to Henry and me de rigueur. We weren't raised that way and we couldn't come to it. So we wore our tails. We noticed in France and Italy that other men wore dinner coats, and we bemoaned our stupidity in bringing our tails and leaving our dinner coats in New York. We fancied in our blindness that on the continent no one noticed the difference. But in England, there doubt disappeared. Whenever we went to an English dinner, in our tails, some

English ladyship through a lorgnette or a spy-glass of some kind gave us the once-over with the rough blade of her social disapproval and we felt like prize boobs suddenly kidnapped from a tacky party and dropped into a grand ball. But we couldn't help it. How should we have known, without our wives to pack our trunks for us in New York, that tails had atrophied in European society and that uniforms and dinner coats had taken their place.

But other things have disappeared from Great Britain since war began, and Henry was doomed to walk the island vainly looking for the famed foods of old England. All through Italy and France, where onion soup and various pastes were served to us, Henry ate them, but in a fond hope that when we got to England he would have some of the " superior comestibles " which a true lover of Dickens had a right to expect. The French were given to ragouts and Latin translations of Mulligan stews, and braised veal smothered in onions and carrots and a lot of staple and fancy green groceries, and these messed dishes irritated Henry. He is the kind of an old-fashioned man who likes to take his food straight. If he eats onions, he demands that they shall be called onions, or if they serve him carrots, he must know specifically that he is eating carrots, and he wants his potatoes, mashed, baked, boiled, or fried and no nonsense about it. Similarly he wants his veal served by itself, and when they bring him a smoking brown casserole of browned vegetables, browned gravy and browned meat, he pokes his fork into it, sniffs, "another cat mess," pushes it aside and asks for eatable food! So all over the continent he was bragging about what he was going to do to "the roast beef of old England," and was getting ready for Yorkshire pudding with it. It was sweet to hear Henry's honest bark at spaghetti and fish-salads, bay deep-mouthed welcome to Sam Weller's "'am and weal pie," and even Pickwick's "chops and tomato sauce," and David Copperfield's toasted muffins, as we drew near the chalk cliffs of England. Also he was going to find what an "eel pie" was, and he had a dozen Dickensonian dishes that he proposed to explore, dishes whose very names would make a wooden Indian's mouth water. But when he got there the cupboard was bare. England was going on rations. Fats were scarce, sugars were rare, starches were controlled by the food board. And who could make a currant tart without these? He dropped two bullet-sized brown biscuits with a hazelnut of butter under

And we felt like prize boobs suddenly kidnapped from
a tacky party and dropped into a grand ball

his vest the first three minutes of our first breakfast and asked for another round, after he had
taken mine.

" That's your allowance, sir," said the waitress,
and money would buy no more.

He noticed a cube of sugar by his coffee cup;
that was his allowance of sugar. We went out to
lunch. Henry ordered the roast beef of old England at the best club in London and got a pink
shaving, escorted in by two boiled potatoes and
a hunk of green cabbage, boiled without salt or
pork. And for dessert we had a sugarless, lard-
less whole-wheat-flour tart! It puckered his
mouth like a persimmon. It fell to me to explain
to Mr. H. G. Wells, who gave the luncheon, that
Henry had just come from the continent, where
he had scorned the food, and one could see from
the twinkle in Mr. Wells's eyes that he was going
to put Henry in a book. And he certainly was a
hero during those London days — the hero of a
great disillusion. Of course the British cooking
was good. The English are splendid cooks, and
they were doing their best; but Henry's picture
of the great boar's head triumphantly borne
into the hall on the shoulders of four stout but-
lers, and his notion of the blazing plum pudding as
large as a hassock, and his preconceived idea of

England as Dickens's fat boy forever stuffing and going to sleep again, had to be entirely revised. For if the English are proud of the way they conceal the bitterness of their sorrow in this war, also they have a vast pride in the way they are sacrificing their creature comforts for it. In Latin countries there is more or less special privilege. But in England, the law is the law and men glory in its rigours by obeying it in proud self-sacrifice. If our dinners sometimes were Spartan in simplicity we found the talk ample, refreshing and filling. We, however, had some trouble with our " Who's Who." One evening they sat me opposite a handsome military man who talked of airships and things most wonderfully and it took me three days to learn that he was the authority on air fighting in Europe! He was a Lord of somewhere, and Earl of something and a Duke of somewhat — all rolled into one. Henry hooted at me for two days. But finally he gave me some comfort. " At least," he said, " you are as well-known in London as your Duke's mixture is in Emporia, and London is a bigger town!" Then it came Henry's turn. At our very grandest dinner they sat Henry between Lord Bryce and one of the most distinguished men of contemporary English letters. Henry shone that night as he never shone before and when Henry turns on his talk he is a wizard. Meredith Nicholson, who has heard Henry talk at a dinner, in a recent number of *Scribner's* magazine, said of him: " He's the best talker I've ever heard. It was delightful to listen to discourse so free, so graphic in its characterization, so coloured and flavoured with the very soil," and that night at the English dinner, all of Henry's cylinders were hitting and he took every grade without changing gears. But my ears were eager for the man on Henry's right. He told some stories; my neck craned toward them. Henry returned the Scotch stories with Kansas stories and held the table.

Then going home in the taxi Henry, recalling his dinner companion, said: " Bill, who was that little man on my left, that man they called Barrie! "

It seemed impossible. Yet those were Henry's very words.

" Henry, Henry, have you never heard of ' Peter Pan,' nor ' The Little Minister,' nor ' Sentimental '—" his friend's answer got no further. Henry's snort of shame almost stopped the taxi.

" No, Bill — no — not that. Well, for Heav-

en's sake! and I sat by him all evening braying
like a jack. Bill — Bill, you won't ever tell this
in Wichita, will you?"

So it must remain forever a secret!

That was a joyful hour for me, but the next
day, Henry had his laugh. We came in from tea
and found a card on the table in the snug little
room near the elevator, which passes for a hotel
office in London. The card was from Lord
Bryce inviting us to tea the next afternoon.
It fell to Henry's lot to go out for the day in the
country, and to me to lunch with Granville Bark-
er. So half-past four saw me rushing into the
hotel from a taxi, which stood waiting outside,
and throbbing up a two-pence every minute.
Then this dialogue occurred.

From me: "Is Mr. Allen in his room?"

From the hall boy: "He is, sir; shall I go for
him, sir?"

From me: "If you will, please, and tell him
I'm in an ungodly hurry, and we have a taxi at the
door chewing up money like a cornsheller!"

The hall boy had to find someone to go on
watch. Time was moving. The tea was at five.
The Bryce apartment was a mile away, and the
chug of that taxi by the door moved me im-
pulsively toward the elevator. But the elevator

was still three steps away, when the manager of the hotel sauntered out from a side door, looked me over leisurely, and asked blandly:

" You'll be going to tea with Lord Bryce this afternoon — I presume!"

My hand was on the elevator button jabbing it fiercely, and my lips replied, " Yes — yes — say — Do you know whether Mr. Allen is in our room? It is getting late and he must hurry or —"

The manager continued to look me over still leisurely, then he smiled persuasively, but spoke firmly; realizing that something would have to be done for the good name of his hotel: " Well now, sir, you wouldn't be wearing those brown shoes to Lord Bryce's tea, would you, Mr. White?" And while that taxi ground out two shillings, black shoes slowly but nervously enveloped two Emporia feet, while Henry stood by and chortled in ghoulish Wichita glee!

But if we made a rather poor fist of our social diversions, at least we had a splendid time at the London shows. And then there was always the prospect of an exciting adventure getting home after the performance was over. The hotel generally found a taxi which took us to the theater. But once there we had to skirmish for ourselves and London is a big town, and hundreds of thousands of Londoners are hunting taxis at eleven at night, and they are hard to catch. So we generally had the fun of walking back to Brook Street in the dark. And it is dark in London toward midnight. Paris is merely gloomy. Rome is a bit somber, but London is as black as the inside of your hat. For London has been bombed and bombed by the German airmen, until London in the prevailing mist which threatens fog becomes mere murk. Night after night we wandered the crooked streets inquiring our way of strangers, some of whom were worse lost than we; one night we took a Londoner in charge and piloted him to Leicester Square; and then got lost ourselves finding Piccadilly and Regent Street! So that whenever we went out after dinner we were never without dramatic excitement, even if it was not adequately supplied by the show. The London taste in shows seems to sheer away from the war. In the autumn last past but two shows had a war motive: One " General Post," a story of the fall of caste from English life during the war, telling how a tailor became a general; the other " The Better 'Ole," a farce comedy, with a few musical skits in it, staged entirely " at the front." " The Better

" Well now, Sir, you wouldn't be wearing those brown
shoes to Lord Bryce's tea, would you, Mr. White?"

'Ole " could be put on in any American town and
the fun would raise the roof! There is no story
to it; the show is but a series of dialogues to illus-
trate Bairnsfather's cartoons.

A soldier comes splashing down the trench.
His comrade cries, " Say, Alf, take yer muddy
feet out o' the only water we got to sleep in."
Again a soldier squats shivering with fear in a
shell hole, while the bombs are crashing over
him, and dirt threatens to bury him. A comrade
looks in and to his captious remarks the squat-
ting soldier answers, " If you knows where
there's a better 'ole, go to it!" Three men
seated on a plum jam box during a terrific bombardment. Trees are falling, buildings crumbling, the landscape heaving, and Bert says, " Alf
— we'll miss this old war wen it's over!" As
the shells strike nearer and nearer and a great
crater yawns at their feet they crawl into it, are
all but buried alive by the dirt from another
shell, and Bert exclaims, " Say, Alf, scare me —
I got the 'iccoughs!" And so it goes for a
whole evening, while Bert, making love to an
interminable string of girls at each place where
he is billeted at the front, gives away scores of
precious lockets with his mother's hair in them,
and Alf tries forever, unavailingly, to make his

cigarette lighter work, and Old Bill dreams of his wife at home who keeps a " pub "!

The prohibitionist in America would probably insist that she keep a soda fountain or a woman's exchange; but no other alterations would be needed to get the play over the footlights in any English speaking town on the globe.

The British soldiers crowd the house where " The Better 'Ole " is given, but their friends don't like it. The raw rollick of the game with death, which is really Shakespearean in its directness and its horse play — like the talk of the soldiers in " Henry IV " or the chaffing of the grave-diggers in " Hamlet," or the common people in any of Shakespeare's plays, offends the British home-staying sense of propriety, and old ladies and gentlemen write to the *Times* about it. But the boys in khaki jam the theater and howl their approval.

Curiously enough in musical programs one finds no prejudice against German music in London as one finds it in Paris. To get Beethoven in Paris one had to lower the windows, close the shutters, pull down the shades and pin the curtains tight. At the symphony concerts in London one can hear not only Beethoven, but Wagner, who is almost modern in his aggressive Teutonism. But the English have little music of their own, and so long as they have to be borrowing they seem to borrow impartially of all their neighbours, the French, the Slavs, the Germans, and the Italians. Indeed, even when British opinion of Russia was at its ebb, the London Symphony Orchestra put in an afternoon with Tschaicovsky's Fourth Symphony. And yet if, in a few months we could form even a vague notion of the public minds of England, and of France, one might say that England seemed more implacable than France. In France, where one heard no music but French and Italian music in the concerts, at the parks, in opera, one heard a serious discussion going on among school teachers about the history to be taught after the war.

Said one side: "Let's tell the truth about this war and its horrors. Let's tell of murdered women and children, of ravished homes, of pillaged cities, of country-sides scourged clear down to their very milestones! Let's tell how German rapacity for land began the war, and kept it up to its awful end."

Says the other side: "Germany is our permanent neighbour. Our children will have to live with Germany, and our children's children to the end of time. War is a horrible thing. Hate breeds war. Why not then let the story of this war and its barbarities die with this generation? Why should we for ever breed hate into the heart of our people to grow eternally into war?"

England has no such questions in her mind. England will surely tell the truth and defy the devil. But the Briton in matters of music and the other arts is like 'Omer when he " smote 'is bloomin' lyre "; the Briton also will go and take what he may require, without much sentiment in the matter.

But the things that roll off the laps of the gods, after humanity has put its destinies there, sometimes are startlingly different from the expected fruits of victory. We fight a war for one thing, win the war and get quite another thing. The great war now waging began in a dispute over spheres of influence, market extensions, Places in the Sun and Heaven knows what of that sort of considerations. Great changes in these matters, of course, must come out of the war. But boundaries and markets will fluctuate with the decades and centuries. The important changes that will come out of this war — assuming that the Allies win it — will be found in the changed relations of men. The changes will be social and economic and they will be institutional and lasting.

For generally speaking, such changes as approach a fair adjustment of the complaints of the " have nots " against the " haves " in life, are permanent changes. Kings, overlords, potentates, politicians, capitalists, high priests — masters of various kinds — find it difficult to regain lost privileges and perquisites. And in this war Germany stands clearly for the " haves." If Germany wins, autocracy will hood its losing ground all over the world. For the same autocracy in Berlin lives in Wall Street, and in the " city " in London, and in the caste and class interests of Italy and France. But junkerdom in Germany alone among the nations of the earth rests on the divine right of kings that is the last resort of privilege. In America we have the democratic weapons to break up our plutocracy whenever we desire to do so. In England they are breaking up their caste and economic privileged classes rapidly. In France and Italy junkerdom is a motheaten relic. And when junkerdom in Germany is crushed, then at least the world may begin the new era, may indeed begin to fight itself free. In the lands of the Allies the autocracy will be weakened by an allied victory. In Germany the junkers will be strong if they win the war, and their strength will revive junkerism all over the earth. If the Allies win, it will weaken junkerdom everywhere. Germany, it is true, treats her working classes better than some of the Allies treat their working people. But it is with the devilish wisdom of a wise slaveholder, who sees profit in fat slaves. The workers get certain legal bonuses. They have economic privileges, not democratic rights of free men under German rule. And the roaring of the big guns out at the front, seemed to Henry and me to be the crashing walls of privilege in the earth.

Of course in this war, while some of the strange things one sees and hears in Europe may pass with the dawn of peace — woman, for instance, may return indoors and come out only on election day, yet unquestionably most of the changes in economic adjustment have come to stay. They are the most important salvage that will come out of the wreck and waste of this war. In England, for instance, the new ballot reform laws are fundamental changes. They provide virtually for universal manhood suffrage and suffrage for women over thirty upon something of the same terms as those provided for men. So revolutionary are the political changes in England that after the war, it is expected — conceded is hardly too strong a word, that the first political cabinet to arise after the coalition cabinet goes, will be a labour cabinet. Certainly if labour does not actually dominate the British government, labour will control it indirectly. And the labour gains during the war will not be lost. Wages in England, and for that matter in most of the allied countries are now being regulated by state ordinance and not by competitive rates. " The labour market " has passed with the slave market. Wages are based not upon supply and demand in labour, but upon the cost of what seems to be a decent standard of subsistence. This change, of course, is fundamental. It marks a new order in the world. And the labour party of England recently adopted a program which provides not merely for the decent living wage for workmen, independent of the " labour market," but also provides for the democratic control of industry: national railways, national mines, national electricity, national housing, and national land tenure. And as if that were not enough the demands of the labour party include the permanent control of the prices of all the necessaries of life, without relation to profits and independent of supply and demand. Such things have been done during the war, and in a crisis. Labour demands that they be done permanently.

And still further to press home its claims upon society, British labour demands a system of taxation levied conspicuously and frankly at the rich to bring their incomes and their holdings only to a moderate rise above the common level — a rise in some relation to the actual differences of mind and heart and soul and service between men, and not a difference based on birth and inheritance and graft and grabbing. It is, of course, revolution. But Labour now has political rights in England, and has time and again demonstrated that it has a majority in every part of the United Kingdom, and it is closely organized and rather determined, and probably will have its way. In France and in Italy where for ten years the Socialists have more or less controlled assemblies and named cabinets, demands like those of the English are being made.

And when the Allies win it will not be so much a change in geography that shall mark off the world of the nineteenth century from the world of the twentieth, as the fundamental social and economic changes in society. The hungry guns out there at the front have eaten away the whole social order that was!

For conditions in this war are new in the world. In every other war, soldiers have dreamed high dreams of their rewards. But they have not taken them — chiefly because their dreams were impractical, somewhat because the dreams that were practical were not held by a majority; or to some extent because if they were held by a majority the majority had no power. Now — even Henry admitted this is no mere theory — we have a new condition. In Europe for two decades the labour problem has been carefully thought out. Labour is in a numerical majority and the majority has political power and political purpose. Labour has been asking and getting about the same things in every country. It has been asking and getting a broader political control in order to assume a firmer economic control.

But one day we read in the London papers of an incident that indicated how far the state control of industry has gone in England. A strike occurred and an important industry was threatened — not over wages, not over hours, not over shop conditions, but over the recognition of the union. Pig-headed managing directors stood firm against recognizing the unions. Then the government stepped in and settled the strike and has compelled the owners of the plant to remove the managing director and to put in men satisfactory to the workers! Labour now is beginning all over Europe to formulate a demand for a place in the directorate of industries. This place in the directorate of industries is demanded that labour may have an intelligent knowledge of the profits of a business so that labour honestly may share those profits with capital. That this condition is coming in Europe no one will deny who sees the rush of events toward a redistribution of the profits of industry.

Having the vision and having the power to get what it desires, only the will to use the power is needed. And that will is motived by the great shadow that is hanging over the world — the shadow of public debt in this war. Someone must pay that debt. Heretofore war debts have fallen heaviest upon the poor. Those least able to pay have paid the most. But those least able to pay are coming out of this war too smart for the old adjustment of the debt. Education, for the past fifty years has made a new man, who will refuse to be over-taxed. During our visit to the front the soldiers were forever saying to Henry and me: " We have offered our lives. Those who stayed at home must give up their riches." And as we went about in England we were always hearing about the wisdom of a heavy confiscatory tax. Among the conservatives them-

selves who presumably have a rather large share
of the national wealth, there is a serious feeling
that immediately after the war a tax-measure
should be passed which would at once confiscate
a certain portion of the property of the country
— one hears different per cents discussed; some
declare that ten per cent is enough, while others
hold that it will require 25 per cent. This confiscatory tax is to be collected when any piece of
property changes hands, and the accruing sum is
to be used for paying off the national debt, or a
considerable portion of it at once. The situation
is completely changed from that which followed
the Napoleonic wars, where war taxes fell largely
upon labour. So in self-preservation, capital is
considering turning over a part of its property to
the state to avoid the slow and disintegrating
grind that otherwise inevitably must come.

A curious side light on the way in which
democracy is conducting this war is found in the
way by which it finances the war. The great
debt of the war, piled up mountain high, is of
course, converted into bonds. These bonds,
similar to our Liberty Bonds, have been pur-
chased not exclusively by the bankers as in
former wars, but by the people of the middle
class and of the labouring class. Thus democ-

racy has its savings in war bonds, which would be wiped out by an indemnity to Germany, but would be greatly inflated by an Allied victory; and where the treasure is, there the heart is! Perhaps it was political strategy which placed the war bonds in the hands of the people. But more than likely it was financial necessity. For the tremendous financial burden of this war was too great for the investing classes to bear unaided. So even the financing of the war has been more or less democratized. In fact, the whole conduct of the war is democratized.

One of the corroborating proofs that this is after all not a king's war, but a people's war, is found in the kind of stories they were forever telling Henry and me about the war. They are not hero stories. Mostly they are funny stories, more or less gently guying the " pomp and circumstance of glorious war," for it is the proud boast of the British army that this is a noncoms' war. Doubtless the stories have small basis in fact, but the currency of these blithe stories reflects the popular mind. Thus they say that when General Haig and his staff came down to review the Canadian troops and pin a carload of hardware on their men for bravery in battle, medals of one sort and another, the Canadian

General lined his huskies up, and as the staff approached he cried anxiously, " Say, boys — here he comes. Now see if you can't stand to attention, and for Heaven's sake, fellows, don't call me Bill while he is here! "   And then they say that after the heavy hardware and shelf goods were distributed a British officer lifted his voice to say: " Men, you have written a brave page upon our history. No more splendid courage than yours ever has been known in the annals of our proud race. But with such magnificent courage, why can you not display other soldierly qualities. Why are you so loose in your discipline? Why don't you treat your officers with more respect? " And in the pause a voice from the ranks replied, " They're not a bad lot, sir. We like 'em all right. But we have 'em along for mascots! "

The French also seem to have their easy-going ways. For current smoking room fiction relates that last spring after a troop of French soldiers had been hauled out to be shot for refusing to go into battle under orders, a whole division revolted and demanded new officers — and got new officers — before they would move forward. And the same smoking room fiction says that in the revolt the men were right and the officers wrong.

" Why," asked a new English officer of some Russian troops who had made a splendid assault on a German position in the spring of 1917, an assault that required high courage and great soldierly skill, " why did you men all lift up your hands just before the charge was made?" The noncom grinned and answered, " We were taking a vote upon the matter of the charge, sir!"

In a theater on the boulevards in Paris recently a hit was made by introducing a stage scene showing the princes and nobility in poverty, looking down from a gallery at the top of the theater, on the rich working people in the boxes below; the princes and nobility were singing a doleful ditty and dancing a sad dance about the changed circumstances that were glooming up the world.

Simultaneously across the channel in England, they were telling this one. Lord Milner, who in Germany would be one of the All Highest of the High Command, was calling at an English house where the children were not used to nobility. They heard their father refer to Lord Milner as " my lord." And one child edged up to him in awe and asked, " O sir, were you indeed born in a manger?" The All Highest smiled and quoth in reply, " No, my child, no, I was not born in a manger, but if they keep on taxing me, I fear I shall die in one!"

The Italians have high hopes of harnessing their nine millions of horsepower in Alpine water-falls, running their state-owned railroads and public utilities with it, and introducing electricity as an industrial power into Italian homes, thus bringing back to the homes of the people the home industries like weaving which steam took away a century ago. But this is only a dream. Yet sometimes dreams do come true. And dreams are wishes unexpressed; and in this day of demo-cratic power, a wish with a ballot behind it be-comes a will, and soon hardens into a fact. The times are changing. But of course human nature remains much the same. Men under a given environment will do about the same kind of things under one set of circumstances. But we should not forget in our computations that laws, customs, traditions, the distribution of wealth, make an en-tirely new environment, and that circumstances are not the same when environment differs. That the surroundings of those people known col-lectively as " the poor " have changed, and changed permanently by the war, no one who sees them in Europe can doubt. They are well-fed, well-housed, and are determined to be well-educated. They know that they can use their ballots to get their share of the wealth they produce. They are never going to be content again with crusts. They are motived now by hope rather than by fear, and they are going to react strangely during the next ten years on the social structure of this old world. But even the new majority will not change everything of course. Grass will grow, water will run down hill, smart men will lead fools, wise men will have the places of honour and power, in proportion to the practicality of their wisdom. But for all that, we shall have in a rather large and certainly in a keenly interesting degree a new heaven and a new earth.

Now as these speculations upon the new order came to us as our journey drew to its close in England, the war seemed slowly to change its meaning. It became something more than a conflict; it seemed to be a revolution — world-wide, and all encompassing. Then we thought of "the front" in new terms.

We realized that behind the curtain in Germany, a despotic will, scientifically guided, is controlling the food, the munitions, the assembling of men and materials for this war. But on this side of the German curtain at the "front" which we knew, a democratic purpose is doing these things. The view of that democratic purpose at work, to me at least, was my chief trophy of the war. The laws which make food conservation possible, which direct shipping, mobilize railroads, control industry, regulate wages, prescribe many of the habits of life to fit the war, all rise out of the experience of the people. There is a vast amount of the " consent of the governed " in this whole war game, so far as the Allies are concerned. And as it is in democratic finance, so also is it in the taste and talent and capacity for war. That also is democratic. What a wide range of human activity is massed in this business of war!

For days and days after we left the continent, in our minds we could see armies moving into the trenches somewhere along the " far flung battle line," and other armies moving out. The picture haunted us. It seemed to me a cinematograph of democracy. For the change of an army division from the trenches, tired, worn and bedraggled, moving wearily to its station of rest, with another army division, fresh and eager, moving up from its station of rest to the front, is indeed a social miracle. It is a fine bit of human machinery. So in terms of our modern democracy it may be well to review the interminable panorama of this democratic war. Fifty years ago it would have been a memorable achievement. Waterloo itself was not such a miracle. Yet somewhere in this war, this wonder is done every day and no record is made of it. Imagine hundreds of miles of wide, white roads, hard-surfaced and graded for the war, leading to a sector of the line. To make and keep these roads, itself is a master's job. Imagine the roads filled all day with two long lines of trucks, passing and repassing; one line carrying its guns and camp outfit, its whole paraphernalia of war, going to the battle front in the hills; another never-ceasing procession with its martial impedimenta coming out of the hills to rest. A few horses hauling big gun carriages straggle through the dust. Here and there, but rarely, is a group of marching men — generally men singing as they march. Occasionally a troop of German prisoners marching with the goose step, comes swinging along carrying their shovels at a martial angle — road menders — which proves that we are more than thirty kilos from the firing line; now and then a camp-kitchen rattles past. But ever in one's ears is the rich rumble of trucks, recalling the voluptuous sound of the circus wagon on the village street. But always there are two great circus parades, one going up, one coming down. Lumbering trucks larger than city house-moving vans whirl by in dust clouds; long — interminably long — lines of these trucks creak, groan and rumble by. Some of the trucks are mysteriously non-committal as to their contents — again reproducing the impression of the circus parade. Probably they hide nothing more terrible than tents or portable ice plants. But most of the trucks that go growling up and come snarling down the great white roads, bear men; singing men, sleeping men, cheering men, unshaved men, natty men, eating men, smoking men, old men and young men, but always cheerful men — private soldiers hurrying about the business of war; to their trenches or from their trenches, but always cheerful. Sometimes a staff officer's car, properly caparisoned, shuttles through the line like a flashing needle; sometimes a car full of young officers of the line tries to nose ahead of the men of the regiment, but rather meekly do these youngsters try to sneak their advantage, as one swiping an apple; no great special privilege is theirs. Interminable lines of truck-mounted guns rattle along, each great gun festively named, as for instance, " The Siren," or " Baby " or

" The Peach " or " The Cooing Dove." Curious snaky looking objects all covered with wiggly camouflage — some artist's pride — are these guns, and back of them or in front of them and around them, clank huge empty ammunition wagons going out, or heavy ones coming in. At short intervals along the road are repair furnaces, and near them a truck or a gun carriage, or an ambulance that has turned out for slight repairs. In the village are great stores of gasoline and rubber, huge quantities of it assembled by some magic for the hour's urgent need.

What a marvel of organization it is; no confusion, no distraught men, no human voice raised except in ribald song. From the ends of the earth have come all these men, all these munitions, all this food and tents and iron and steel and rubber and gas and oil. And there it centers for the hour of its need on this one small sector of the front; indeed on every small sector of the long, long trail, these impedimenta of war come hurrying to their deadly work. And it is not one man; not one nation even, not one race, nor even one race kindred that is assembling this endless caravan of war. It is a spirit that is calling from the vasty deep of this world's treasure, unto material things to rise, take shape and gather at this tryst with death. It is the spirit of democracy calling across the world. The supreme councils of the Allies — what are they? They change, form and reform. Generals, field marshals, staff officers in gold lace, cabinets, presidents, puppet kings, and God knows what of those who strut for a little time in their pomp of place and power — what are they but points on the drill of the great machine whose power is the people of the world, struggling in protest against despotism, privilege, autocracy and the pretence of the few to play greedily at the master game. The points break off, or are worn off — what difference does it make? Joffre, French, Cardona, Neville, Asquith, Painleve, Kitchener, Haig — the drill never ceases; the power behind it never falters. For once in the world the spirit of democracy is organized; organized across lines of race, of language, of national boundary! A score of million men, in arms, a score of billions of people — workers, captains of industry, local leaders, little governors and commercial princelets, bosses, farmers, bankers, skilled labourers, and men and women of fumbling hands and slow brains, teachers, preachers, philosophers, poets, thieves, harlots, saints and sinners — all the free people of the world, giving what talents Heaven has bestowed upon them to make the power of this great machine that moves so smoothly, so resistlessly, so beautifully along the white ribbons of roads up to the battle.

When the battle ceases, of course, that organization will depart. But always democracy will know that it can organize, that it can rise to a divine dignity of courage and sacrifice. And that knowledge is the great salvage of this war. More than written laws, more than justice established, more than wrongs righted in any nation, and in all the nations will be the knowledge of this latent power of men!

CHAPTER IX

WE found when we were leaving England another of those curious contrasts between the nations of the earth that one meets in a long journey. Coming into Bordeaux we were convoyed for three hours by a ratty little French destroyer and a big dirigible French balloon. Leaving Liverpool, we lay two nights and a day sealed in the harbour, and then sailed out with the *Arabic,* the *Mongolian,* the *Victorian,* and two freighters, amid a whole flock of cruisers and destroyers. The protecting fleet stayed with us two nights and three days. On the French boat the barber practically had no news of sudden deaths and hairbreadth escapes which had happened while we slept. We sailed into the Gironde River peacefully, almost joyously. But we left the Mersey with a story that a big fleet of destroyers hovered at the river's mouth; that the *Belgic* had been beached out there on a shoal by a "sub," and that we would be lucky if our throats were not cut in the water as we tried to swim ashore after we had been blown out of our boats.

The French certainly are more casual than the English. But then, the Germans have sunk virtually no French liners, while the British liner is the favourite food of von Tirpetz! They even showed us his teeth marks on our American liner, the *New York*. On an earlier trip during the summer of 1917 the boat had been torpedoed when Admiral Sims was a passenger, going to England. The Admiral was sitting at dinner when the explosion occurred and the force of it threw him to the high ceiling of the dining saloon! At least that's what they told us. Caution and conflicting doubts, " fears within and foes without," were not so unreasonable as one might fancy, coming out of any British port.

But to Henry and me the greatest contrast came, not in the conduct of the ship's officers, as compared with the French seamen, but in the ship's company, going to war and coming away from it. We went with youth; the *Espagne* was crowded with young men going to war, with young women going out to serve those who were salvaging the waste of war. The boat carried a score of lovers — some married, some impromptu,

some incidental and fleeting, but all vastly interesting. For when the new wine blooms the old
ferments, and stumbling over the dark decks at
night on the *Espagne,* we were forever running
into youth paired off and gazing at the mystery
of the ocean and the stars. So the corks were
always popping in our old hearts; and we enjoyed it. But we paced the black night decks of
the *New York* as " one who treads alone a ban-
quet hall deserted." We were among the younger
people on the ship. There was no youth to play
with under thirty! No one touched the piano.
No one lifted his voice in song. The most devilish thing going as we sailed was a game of chess!
There was a night game of whist or cribbage or
some other sedentary game, which closed at ten,
and after that in the library the talk sagged and
died like a decomposed chord in a Tschaikovsky
symphony! It was sad! One had to go to the
smoking room where there was wassail on lemon
squash and insipid English beer until after midnight. But there the talk was good. Of course
it sometimes bore a strong smell of man about it,
but it was virile and wise. A rug dealer from
Odessa, a dealer in mining machinery from Moscow, a Chicago college professor returning from
Petrograd, a cigarette maker from Egypt, a brace

of British naval officers going over to return with Canadian transports, an American aerial engineer, back from an inspection trip to France, a great English actor, who once played Romeo with Mary Anderson — to give one an approximate of his age — a Red Cross commission from Italy, and an Australian premier. The whole ship's company was but thirty-four first class and of these but six were women. It was no place for dashing young blades in their late forties like Henry and me.

As the hour for leaving the ship approached, the press of the splendid months behind us drew Henry and me together more and more. We were hanging over the deck rail looking at a faint attempt at a cloudy sunset at the end of our last day out. We fell to talking of the love affairs on the *Espagne,* and perhaps from me came some words about the Eager Soul, the Gilded Youth and the Young Doctor. Henry looked up dazed and anxious. Clearly he did not know what it was all about.

" Who was this Gilded Youth? " asked Henry.

" He was the dream we dreamed when we were boys, Henry. When fate set you out as a book agent on the highway and me to kicking a Peerless job press in a dingy printing office. The

Gilded Youth was all we would fain have been!"

"And the Eager Soul?" quoth he.

"She, dearly beloved, was the ideal of our boyish hearts. Did you ever have a red-headed sweetheart in those olden golden days, Henry?" He shook a sad head in retrospection. "Nor did one ever come to me. But most boys want one sometime, so I took her off the Red Cross Posters and breathed the breath of life into her. And isn't she a peach; and doesn't she kind of warm your heart and make up for the hardship of your youth?" He smiled assent and asked: "But the young Doctor, Bill, surely he —"

"He is the American spirit in France, Henry — badly scared, very shy at heart, full of hope and dying to serve!"

"And it never happened — any of it?" asked Henry.

"Yes, oh, yes, Henry. There was the tall boy who played Saint Saens on the *Espagne,* and did the funny stunt at the auction; there was the night we sat on the food box near the front at Douaumont and heard the ambulance boy whistling the bit from "Thais," far up the hill in the misty moonlight; there was the French soldier by the splintered tree in the Forest of Hess; there was the head nurse killed by the abri between

Souilly and Verdun, who waited while her girls went in; there was the poor dying boy in the hospital for whom you bought the flowers and there was the handsome New York woman coming over to start her hospital. There was the young doctor whom the German officer prisoner tried to kill. And there was the picture of the red-headed Red Cross nurse, and there were our dreams."

" And the ending — will you have a happy ending? " demanded Henry.

" Aren't the visions of the young men, and the dreams of the old always happy? It is in passing through life from one to the other that our courage fails and our hearts sadden. And these phantoms are of such stuff as dreams are made of and they may not falter or grow weary, or grow old. Youth always has a happy ending — even in death. It is when youth ends in life that we may question its happiness."

And so we left our fancies and walked to the big guns far forward and gazed into the sunset, where home lay, home, and the things that were real, and dear, and worth while.

THE END

APPENDIX A

A Soldier's Song

Love, though these hands that rest in thine so
Love, though our dreams shall have no hope but

dear, Back in-to dust, may crum-ble
this, Love, though our faith must be our

with the year; Love, though these lips, that
rar-est bliss; Love, though the years may

PRINTED IN THE UNITED STATES OF AMERICA

THE following pages contain advertisements of Macmillan books by the same author.

God's Puppets

By William Allen White

Cloth, 12mo, with Frontispiece, $1.35

"Five capital stories full of scorn for hypocrisy, meanness and anti-social types of character, and of equal admiration for men who are clean, straight and generous. The book has the tone and purpose of Mr. White's 'A Certain Rich Man.' It has also humour and a closely drawn picture of small town conditions in the Middle West."— *Outlook.*

"Literature that is lifelike in essence, moral without being hypocritical, dramatic without being theatricalized, inspiring without being preachy."— *New York Sun.*

"You will not very often find a writer who, with as little apparent technical finesse, makes his characters so palpably alive and vigorous."— *Harper's Weekly.*

"Mr. White's psychology . . . is always subtle, but it is always truthful, and he is able to exhibit it in a well-contrived plot."— *New York Evening Post.*

"'The One a Pharisee' is a great short story. It gets down to fundamentals, deals with them directly and sanely, and has unexpected beauty. The other stories are excellent; they have holding power and verities, they are graphic, vivid, and well-built, with colloquial expressiveness and pungent accuracy. . . . 'God's Puppets' is a definite and noteworthy accomplishment."— *Bellman.*

THE MACMILLAN COMPANY
Publishers 64–66 Fifth Avenue New York

A VIEW OF AMERICAN DEMOCRACY

The Old Order Changeth

By WILLIAM ALLEN WHITE

Cloth, 12mo, $1.25

This is a collection of stirring essays on topics of present-day interest. Opening with a discussion of the former democracy of this country, the author considers the beginnings of the change, the cause and certain definite tendencies. "Schools," Mr. White says, "are the mainspring of democracy" and "courts the check." Startling as this assertion may seem, he backs it up with a number of arguments which would appear to be conclusive. The last chapter he has entitled *A Look Ahead,* and the volume closes with these inspiring words:

"We of this generation have done somewhat to solve the problems that steam has brought to us. And we are by no means done with our day's work. Indeed, it is but dawn in the new day of spiritual awakening. Let us touch those who, still sleeping, wear the joy of youth upon their faces, and say, with the prophet of old:

"'Arise, shine; for thy light is come and the glory of the Lord is risen upon thee.'"

THE MACMILLAN COMPANY
Publishers   64–66 Fifth Avenue   New York